C. M. Russell, "The Cowboy Artist."

C. M. R.

CHARLES M. RUSSELL
Cowboy Artist

C.M.R.

CHARLES M. RUSSELL
Cowboy Artist

7580

A BIOGRAPHY by AUSTIN RUSSELL

TWAYNE PUBLISHERS

New York

To my sister, who first suggested that
I write this book.

Copyright 1957, by Austin Russell

MANUFACTURED IN THE UNITED STATES OF AMERICA
UNITED PRINTING SERVICES, INC.
NEW HAVEN, CONN.

FOREWORD

Charles Marion Russell, the Cowboy Artist, was my uncle and when I was young I lived with him for years both at his Great Falls home and his summer camp, Bull's Head Lodge, up in the Rockies. I went with him on pack-trips, and when he and Nancy, his wife, were away I batched in his log cabin studio.

That was before the first World War, and now Joe DeYong and I are the only people left alive who knew Charlie intimately by dint of living under his roof. We helped him pack, and make and break camp, and chop firewood, and fetch water. We saw him, as few did, when he got grumpy, which is to say when he was fighting a picture—for sometimes his pictures fought back and wouldn't be painted.

And we, I think, were the only people for whom Charlie quit the home range and painted pictures of Huns and Tartars and Aztecs and Romans. But this, of course, was mere byplay, not to be taken seriously.

In his own field—the northern plains Indians and the cattlemen—Charlie was as accurate a historian as Catlin, a century earlier. He never romanticized his subject: he never improved on his punchers and Indians—he painted them as they were.

I have tried to do the same sort of job with this biography. It has not been novelized or fictionalized in any way: there are no invented incidents or conversations, and there is no plot except the course of Charlie's life.

January, 1957   AUSTIN RUSSELL.

TABLE OF CONTENTS

1

When Cattlemen Ruled From Canada To Mexico (The 1880's)

High noon on the high prairie, in the distance a flat-topped butte as red as paint, sun shining, rocks glowing, breeze blowing, grass flowing, and Charlie Russell, twenty-two years old—as slim as a boy, as blonde as a Swede, and burned as brown as an Indian—riding "outer circle," looking for strays which had got away from the herd.

In every beef herd there are always a few solitary, hermit-minded steers, blighted beings who wander off by themselves, and—like "rogue elephants" in Ceylon—these are always the most ugly and dangerous. They want to be left alone, to go where the grazing takes them, to drift before the wind; they resent intruders; and a steer, with his needle-pointed horns, is better equipped than most neurotics to implement his resentment.

Riding down a deep draw with sharp bends in it, blue shadows under the overhang, and pinnacle rocks like a miniature bad-lands, Charlie came suddenly on one of these hermits, a big longhorn in a vicious state of mind.

The steer, ruminating, had heard hoofs coming and was prepared; Charlie wasn't. The first Charlie knew of the steer was when he heard an angry snort and his horse shied.

Before he could unloop his rope the steer jumped him, got him in the cut, and crowded him right up against the bank.

A good cow-horse would have slipped out of it with a quick stop and a whirl-around backwards, but Charlie was breaking in a new pony and it got rattled and shied sideways up against the rock. There was no room to swing the rope and Charlie had no quirt.

There was only one thing to do.

The near horn was about to gut his horse when Charlie pulled his gun—got it out just in time—and reached over, arm's length, and shot straight down right through the steer's head. It was a forty-five and though it didn't touch the brain part of the skull—just went through the nose bone—the impact of the heavy bullet almost knocked the steer flat. It spraddled out wide, all fours, and shook its head—it must have been badly powder-burned—the most astonished animal in all Montana. It probably thought—if a steer thinks—that it had been hit by lightning. Then it wobbled off sideways, still shaking its head.

The bullet had made a clean hole right through the nose bone, the tongue, and the lower jaw, and thick black smoke was still streaming out of the wound both above and below. Charlie sat in the saddle watching and was surprised at how much smoke came out and how long it kept coming.

It was before the First World War that I heard my uncle, Charlie Russell, tell this, and even now, after all these years, I can see it like a picture: Charlie sitting there in the saddle with both hands up nearly shoulder high, in one the reins, in the other the forty-five—it too still smoking—he and his horse both watching the steer stagger off; and behind them the pinnacle rocks and the shadow under the cutbank— bright blue shadow—and the shelving slope on which the pony stood, and the sun streaming down; I can see it all in detail.

When Cattlemen Ruled (The 1880's)

There was magic in Charlie's talk: he made you see things. And yet *he* told none of this in detail—*you* just saw it. Of course, for your mind's eye to fill in the background you had to know the country.

And he, and his horse, and the steer, dead years and years ago, and nothing left anywhere now to show for their meeting. Unless indeed, as some people believe, the record thereof—like the record of everything else that ever happened—is still somewhere in the universe. Still there and ready for us to read as soon as we learn how.

All this sounds like the start of a two-gun western but is really just one of the thousand things that Charlie saw while he was still punching cows; saw it more vividly than you and I would see it: and painted it later, when he became Charles M. Russell, the Cowboy Artist.

2

The Russell Farm—As Big, Almost,
As A Barony

Charles Marion Russell, who wound up in Montana as the Cowboy Artist, began life in St. Louis as a problem child: not bad, not vicious, not even as cruel as most boys—he was too fond of animals—but he just wouldn't stay in school.

Inspired by his father reading aloud, he did learn to read and write, and devoured Mayne Reid, Harry Castleman and other early writers of boys' books, but reading and writing was as far as he got. Why bother learning long division and how to parse a sentence when he intended to go out West and fight Indians?

Born during the Civil War, on March 19, 1864, Charlie spent most of his childhood on the old Russell farm at Oak Hill—which was then outside St. Louis but is now in it. It was an enormous place, stretching from west of Kingshighway right to Grand Avenue, from Arsenal Street to the Gravois Road. (With all that land the family should have grown rich but didn't.) When Charlie was born, it had been divided among the four children of James Russell—three Russell families, one Parker—and they still had a patch of forest of their own called Grandma's Woods. Each family had a big brick house—big for those days—on the highest part of Oak Hill. They could see for miles in every direction.

Besides cornfields and pastures and pear and apple orchards, they had a large stone wine house and vineyards which reached almost to Grand Avenue, and made so much wine that they sold it in barrels, not in bottles. They had also, right on the farm, a pond which they called The Lake—as if it was the only one—with a home-made boat in it, and even a home-made island. They had also, right on the farm, a coal and fireclay mine—coal and clay often go together in overlapping seams—a company store for the miners, and the works or "diggin's," a pattern-shop, a brick shed, a pug-mill, and a street of old fashioned bee-hive kilns with domes like an oriental village.

The three Russell brothers and their Parker brother-in-law called themselves the Parker-Russell Mining and Manufacturing Co., and their sons and grandsons kept the firm going for seventy-four years.

Altogether the old Russell farm was an ideal place for some twenty active cousins of all sizes.

Besides the cousins, for playing—and fighting—purposes, there were the kids from the "diggin's," the children of Welsh miners, come all the way from the Old Country; people who still said thee and thou and had queer un-American names like Wagstaff and Woodruff and Holdsworth—but they pronounced it 'Oldsworth.

One of the Wagstaffs told Charlie, "Thou art a rare blade."

He wasn't quoting anything—that was the way he talked. Charlie never forgot it.

Yet there was no danger of the kids growing up to be hill billies and saying "hit" for "it," as country people still do in Missouri.

Right there, in plain sight across the mile-wide hollow of the Mill Creek Valley, was St. Louis—a smudge of soft-coal smoke by day, a dull glow of coal-gas lamps by night—the metropolis of the whole Mississippi-Missouri River country, the biggest city, barring New Orleans, west of Cincinnati, with schools and universities—one Catholic, one Protestant—

and hospitals and breweries, and factories and horse-cars, and even an art gallery, and everything that goes to make a city.

Oak Hill is not very far from the Grant Farm, and before the war Charlie's father, Charles Russell, Sr. had often seen U. S. Grant hauling mine-props on the Gravois Road. At that time, Grant—though a hero of the Mexican War—was considered a drunk and a failure; by the time Charlie was big enough to notice such things Grant was President.

The Russells had a church of their own at Oak Hill, built by the four families—Presbyterian originally, but one of the uncles married an Episcopalian and she changed the church to suit and called it Holy Innocents; and the other brothers and sisters-in-law were such gunnies that they let her get away with it.

The great flood of Catholic immigration—and Catholic babies—had just begun, but the country was predominantly Protestant, and people were still on intimate terms with Holy Writ. Sunday mornings the Russells went to church, Sunday afternoons the family assembled in the living-room and the children took turns reading aloud from the Bible. Charlie's elder brother Bent, struggling phonetically with the big words and hard names of the Old Testament, produced one of those long-lasting family jokes—"Pee-Harry-O of Egg-wiped" meaning Pharoah of Egypt.

Another Sunday, reading from the New Testament, Bent did even better—"He re-bucked the waves and there fell a great clam."

The re-bucked waves—flattened over backwards—and the great clam falling slowly from the heavens make a solemn and impressive picture. It fell, you feel sure, amid an awful silence, lit with a lurid light.

Insensibly, Protestantism was beginning to wear thin. The ladies of the family really believed: the men were more or less Unitarian; they went to church but with reservations. The children just as a matter of course went to both church and Sunday School. They were inoculated but it didn't take: Charlie grew up without any particular religion.

Charlie must have been an odd-looking little kid, sturdily built, as blonde as a Swede—so blonde that from a distance he seemed to have no eyebrows, though, really he had heavy ones—with fierce blue eyes and a stubborn mouth; and he was just as active as his brothers and cousins with nothing whatever to show that he was an artist. Nothing except that he was forever drawing and modeling animals in beeswax and bread crumbs. (They had no modeling wax then, or plasticene, or anything like that.) But the family paid little attention to this because Charlie had an Aunt Sue, an elder sister, also named Sue, and a younger brother Wolfert, all all of whom drew just as well as he did.

Wolfert drew better. I still have his sketchbook filled with girls and horses, and his drawings at seventeen were superior to anything Charlie did until he was nearly thirty. (The name Wolfert came from a New Amsterdam ancestor, Wolfert Ecker—originally Acker—of Wolfert's Roost on the Hudson. See Washington Irving, who lived at Wolfert's Roost and renamed it Sunnyside.) But Wolfert Russell died of typhoid at nineteen. Every family in those days had somebody die of typhoid or smallpox or yellow-jack; and in Swamp-east Missouri thousands lived all their lives to the tune of chills-and-fever, which is to say malaria.

Do you remember Dickens' *American Notes* and the stress he lays on malaria? Some historians think it was slowly spreading malaria that ruined first Greece and then Rome; but on the Mississippi, as the country settled up, the fever seemed to recede.

Charlie's elder brother, Silas Bent Russell (another family name, but he suppressed the Silas and signed himself S. Bent), a tall, slim kid, also with blue eyes—but his were speculative rather than fierce—intended to be, and eventually became, an engineer. As a boy he was always tinkering with gadgets. Reading somewhere that evaporation causes coolness, he rigged up two umbrellas over his bed, and two watering-pots with counter-weights to sprinkle them and a complicated system of gutters to carry off the excess moisture, which—as he learned by experiment—didn't evaporate. It took him only two hours to get to bed, and once in he couldn't get out. Long afterwards his wife remarked, "When I heard about the umbrellas I should, right there and then, have refused to marry him."

But wives, of course, were far in the future, and Charlie and Bent and their younger brothers, Ed and Guy and Wolfert, foresaw as little as anybody else what rows they had to hoe.

Ed and Guy, next in age after Charlie, had an Irish nurse and spoke with a brogue which they didn't get over till they started to school.

Here is Charlie's memory—painted many years later—of the Russell house at Oak Hill. And here—and probably more accurate in its proportions—is Bent's.

⤙ 3 ⤚

How Three Ancestors Got Scalped

Recently, in a box of old photographs, I found this statement, dated Aug. 4, 1911, by Charlie's father, C. S. Russell. He did not sign it and gives no reason but apparently it was written for somebody who intended to write Charlie's biography.

"My father's father came from Rockbridge County, Virginia, in which County my father (James Russell) was born.

"The family later moved to Tennessee when my father was still a boy. When quite a young man my father left home and at one time taught school. At another time he lived in Cape Girardeau where he edited a paper.

"My uncle, William Russell, coming from a family of ten brothers and two sisters, moved to St. Louis about 1805. He bought a farm then located in St. Louis County, from a family named Rector.

"After my uncle William had settled in St. Louis, my father (James) followed him, coming here about 1811. He bought the farm from his brother William which contained 432 acres comprising the original Oak Hill Property.

"My mother, Lucy Bent Russell, advanced part of the money paid for the farm and 100 acres of the property remained in her name. This 100 acres is now known as the L. B. Russell Estate Company property.

"My father's first wife died before he came to St. Louis. Soon after moving and when about forty years old, my father married Lucy Bent who was then about twenty.

17

"My father had at one time practically closed the sale of his farm. One Sunday morning after quite a storm, he went out for a walk around the place expecting to sign the papers to dispose of his farm the next day. The storm had caused the earth to wash in places and he discovered an outcrop of coal near what is now Tholozan Ave. just east of Morganford Road. When the purchaser came the next day to close the deal, my father told him that he had decided not to sell. Soon after this he opened up a coal mine with a drift where the first outcrop was found. He continued mining coal till the time of his death.

"During this period he used to sell coal in St. Louis and used to have it hauled down town by ox team. (As slow as the grace of God. Put both your hands flat on your knees: slide one forward as far as the wrist, then draw it back: slide the other forward etc.—*that's* how oxen walk. They never do more than walk.)

"The city at that time extended as far west as about 4th Street and a little north of the present Court House. (Oak Hill extended from Grand Avenue [36th Street] to Kingshighway [50th Street] and beyond, so it was a long haul. They had to circle Chouteau's Pond and cross the Millcreek Valley.)"

Charlie's father, Charles Silas Russell (1833-1917) looked something like the pictures of Porfirio Diaz, the Mexican dictator, who was almost pure Indian. This led their neighbors, the Compton family, to believe the Russells had Indian blood; but there is no hint of it in the family tree, and the only other Russell who looked Indian was Charlie himself. By middle age he had the high cheekbones, little eyes—at least they looked little after a lifetime of squinting against the prairie sun—heavy jaw, hard mouth, short neck, square shoulders, and well-built body that marked the oldtime Indian. But none of this showed as a child, and he was much the blondest of the family, his hair and eyelashes

18

being almost white. Even in maturity he had almost no hair on his body: he was as smooth as a statue. Which is also very Indian.

Charlie did have halfbreed cousins—one of them an outlaw with a price on his head—a great uncle who was a squawman, and two other uncles who got scalped. Two centuries earlier a third member of the family had been scalped.

These were Charlie's ancestors, the Bents.

In 1638 (eighteen years after the *Mayflower*) a certain John Bent came from Penton-Grafton, southwest of London, and settled in Sudbury, Massachusetts. His son, Peter Bent, had his house burnt and his son scalped in King Philip's War. After this Peter Bent returned to England but his family remained in America.

In 1804, just after the Louisiana Purchase, Peter Bent's great-great-grandson, Silas Bent, a Massachusetts lawyer, came on horseback and flatboat by way of Ohio and Virginia —where he married Martha Kerr—to Saint Louis, Missouri. By 1809 he was Presiding Judge of the Louisiana Territory, and from 1813 to his death in 1827 he was Chief Justice of the Missouri Territory.

This Judge Silas Bent had eleven children, and in 1826 his daughter, Lucy Bent, married James Russell of St. Louis, and became Charlie Russell's grandmother. (In the book of the Bent genealogy Lucy's husband is called Joseph Russell, but this is a misprint: the family Bible gives James.)

St. Louis was as far west as Lucy went, but her brothers, the Bent boys went farther—and fared worse. Their story is tragic, and much too long to give here (it is given in detail in *Bent's Fort* by David Lavender) but what happened to them and their children had such an effect on their St. Louis nephew, Charlie Russell, that to tell *his* story it is necessary to tell theirs. Because what the Bents did—and what was done

19

to them—explains how Charlie felt about the whites and the Indians. And *that* affected his art: he never, except on order, painted American soldiers killing American Indians.

A list of dates tells the main story:—

1816. George Bent, second son of Judge Silas Bent, went west for the Missouri Fur Co. into what is now Montana. These were the days when the famous Hudson Bay Co. of Canada—as powerful as the big corporations are now—was fighting the American companies, and they were fighting each other. The Bents, small fry, were soon driven south.

1821. Mexico freed itself from Spain.

1826. Lucy Bent married James Russell in St. Louis, and that same year her brothers, Charles, George, William, and Robert Bent, built their first trading post in what was then Kansas but is now Colorado.

1832. They founded Bent's Fort on the Arkansaw River, which was for years the largest and most important trading post in the U.S.A. It had 'dobe walls four feet thick and fifteen high, two thirty-foot watch-towers with cannon, and over the main gate a square belfry with a small telescope. It had also a big walled corral for horses and oxen. (The Bents were the first to use freight-wagons instead of pack trains—you don't have to unload a freight-wagon every night as you do a pack-horse.)

Besides the people who lived at the Post, the Bents employed one hundred trappers. Kit Carson ran one of their wagon-trains. It was from Fort Bent that the U.S. army officers, Kearney and Doniphan, started their historic march to Santa Fe and the Pacific, one of the Bents acting as guide.

While they were building the post, the Mexican peons brought the smallpox. William caught it but lived through—pockmarked for life—and warned the Cheyenne Indians away. He had already great influence with the tribe, and, later, he helped to keep them out of the Civil War. For a time he was Indian Agent. He married Owl Woman, a full-blood

Cheyenne, whose father was White Thunder, the keeper of the sacred bundle of "Medicine Arrows." These magic arrows (two Buffalo Arrows—they meant Meat—two Man Arrows—they meant War) played a part in dividing the tribe and led to their migrating south.

1835. Charles Bent, William's elder brother, married Maria Ignacia Jaramillo. Her sister Josefa was Kit Carson's wife. (I don't know whether they were the same family, but a Spaniard, Captain Jaramillo, wrote the memoirs of Coronado's Kansas expedition in 1541.)

1837. Charles Bent was imprisoned by Mexicans. Ignacia dug up seven thousand dollars from the 'dobe floor and ransomed him.

1838. F. Laboue wrote in barbarous French to Papin at Fort Pierre, "Dear Friend, if I had to give you details of all the bastards that are here in the Fort, I would not have enough paper in all Fort Laramie." His horses are in miserable shape, he is short-handed, he wants alcohol, "as much as you can send," and William Bent has been causing trouble. The Bents' own partner, Ceran St. Vrain, was another Frenchman. In those days St. Louis Frenchmen were all over the place, like you know what.

1841. Robert, youngest of the Bent brothers, left the wagon train to shoot a buffalo for meat and was scalped by the Comanches.

1847. Charles, the eldest brother, was the first Civil Governor of New Mexico under the Stars and Stripes. This was just after we seized the country and, naturally, the Mexicans didn't like us.

On his new job, Charles Bent made three refusals, and the third was fatal.

First, though warned Taos was dangerous, he refused a military escort and went there with his family.

Second, he refused to free some Mexicans who were being held for trial.

Third, that night a mob gathered and tried to break in, and Charles refused to open the door. Instead he asked through the door: "What do you want?"

Tomasito, the local bad man, answered: "We want your head!"

Charles still wouldn't open, so they shot him—through the door—broke it in, filled him full of arrows, and scalped him. His ten-year-old son, Alfredo, kept saying, "Let's fight them, Papa!"

While this was happening, Ignacia and the other women dug a hole through the 'dobe wall with a poker and a big iron spoon and crawled through with the children into the next house.

Charles pulled three arrows out of his face and crawled through after them. He died there of his wounds. The insurrectos did not kill Ignacia and the children but they scalped her brother, Pablo Jaramillo.

When at last the soldiers came, George Bent was foreman of the jury. Sixteen were hanged in Taos: but they didn't hang Tomasito—a U.S. dragoon shot him through the head.

William Bent and his squaw Owl Woman had four halfbreed children: Mary, Robert, George, and Charles.

To keep them from growing up as tribal savages they were educated in St. Louis and lived there with their aunt, Dorcas Bent Carr. (*Her* grandaughter, Anne Eliot Clendenin, later married Charlie Russell's elder brother, the engineer.) This Aunt Dorcas and her husband, Judge William Chiles Carr—who built the first brick house in St. Louis and gave Carr Park to the City and rode horseback all the way to Washington to get a charter for the first public school—lived in southern splendor with slaves and blooded racehorses—but Judge Carr freed his slaves long before Lincoln. A splendor which must have been hard on little halfbreed cousins raw from the wilds of the Arkansaw, and may have had something to do with turning Charles—the youngest—into an outlaw. Mary, the eldest, grew up to marry a saloon keeper. Later a still younger half-sister, Julia, married another halfbreed and went back and lived with the Indians. Tribal life had its charms.

Meanwhile their father, William Bent, and his brothers and their partner, Ceran St. Vrain, prospered mightily; their wagon trains and their pack trains and their traders and storekeepers—for they built more than one trading post—covered a territory which now includes seven states. The adobe empire David Lavender calls it. They had also enormous land grants.

Owl Woman had died in giving birth to Charles, Jr. (later the outlaw), and was buried, Indian fashion, in a tree: and William married her younger sister, Yellow Woman, and had the daughter Julia mentioned above, who married the halfbreed Ed Guerrier. She would not be the only one of the family to turn Indian.

1847. A bad year for the Bents. Charles, the Governor, was killed in Taos, and George, the second brother, died at Bent's Fort.

1849. Was worse. The Bent, St. Vrain & Co. partnership broke up. Cholera, brought by the Forty-niner gold rush, killed half of William's people, the Southern Cheyenne, among them Owl Woman's mother, old White Thunder's wife. She too was buried in a tree scaffold grave.

1849. The U.S. army wanted to buy Bent's Fort and make it into an army post, but they wouldn't pay William's price —sixteen thousand dollars—so he blew up the magazine and built a smaller place a few miles down the river. Why he burned the Fort is a mystery. (Later, 1852, he built a large stone fort at Big Timbers.) William's son, George Bent 2nd, said the old Bent's Fort was burned the same year, 1852.

1860. Mary Bent, the eldest daughter, married R. M. Moore and bore William's first grandchild.

1861. William Bent was loyal during the Civil War. He opposed Albert Pike, author of "Dixie," and kept the Cheyennes quiet, but his own halfbreed sons, George and Charles, Jr. though both under age, joined the Confederates.

1862. George Bent, Jr. captured at the battle of Corinth.

1863. When William Bent was living on the Purgatoire River—The River of Lost Souls (*El Rio de Las Animas Perdidas en Purgatorio*)but American cowboys called it the Picketwire—his halfbreed sons, George and Charles, left him to join the Indians.

1864. Charlie Russell, the artist, born in St. Louis.

1865. Alfredo Bent, son of Governor Charles, murdered in Taos by a Mexican called Greek George. Alfredo's children and his sisters Estafina and Teresina sold their share of the land-grant for eighteen thousand dollars. It was soon resold for six hundred and fifty thousand, and, almost immediately, resold again to an English Syndicate for twice that.

1865. Indian war. See halfbreed Robert Bent's account of what he saw soldiers do to Indian women and children. (Item: a little girl, six years old, buried in the sand to hide her. Two soldiers dug her out and shot her. There were also some fancy mutilations and rippings up. Item: Three children —who had somehow escaped being killed—were exhibited in a cage at a Denver carnival. This was a bit too raw and the U.S. Government ransomed them.) Kit Carson, by then a brigadier general, told the army that Col. Bent knew more about the Indians than he did. William offered to guarantee with his life that he could get all the tribes at peace within three months. While he was doing this, General Connor's Pawnee Scouts caught William's wife, Yellow Woman, near Powder River and scalped her and killed her.

1867. Halfbreed George Bent quit his younger brother Charles (the outlaw) and helped to gather the tribes for another vain treaty. (Vain because the whites broke it.)

How Three Ancestors Got Scalped

Charles Bent—no doubt the Cheyennes called him Cholly: just as the Crees and Blackfoot did Charlie Russell, "Cholly, my friend"—though educated in St. Louis as a white man, had also been initiated into a tribal secret society, The Dog Soldiers, and now, after the army made a particularly brutal massacre of Cheyenne women and children, he repudiated the whites and turned Indian. Though only nineteen years old—according to the Bent genealogy he may have been only seventeen—Charles Bent was already a leader and led the Dog Soldiers in a raid on Downer's Stage Station and tortured and mutilated and killed. A contemporary called him, "The worst desperado the plains have ever seen." Governor Gilpin outlawed him and put a price of five thousand dollars on his head. His father disowned him.

Mary, his elder sister, still put a candle in the window to signal Charles: but when at last he came it was not to see Mary. An issue of *Harper's Magazine*, in 1869 gives William's account of it, "My daughter saw something that looked like an Indian's head sticking up over the bank of the irrigating ditch. It was Charley.——he said he was after the Old Man, meaning me. I was off in New Mexico——she asked the durn'd scoundrel to come to the house. 'No' he said, 'I only wanted the Old Man,' and he uncocked his rifle and went away. That's the last we've seen of him."

1868. Charles was wounded in a tribal battle with the Pawnees. The wound did not heal and he died—it is said of malaria—in camp. With his influence over the Indians he was evidently a much more dangerous person than the famous Billy the Kid; but who ever heard of Charley Bent the Breed?

1869. Custer massacred the Cheyennes on the Washita River—some of the tribe, joining the Sioux, were to help kill Custer at the Little Big Horn—and shortly after, William Bent, leading one of his wagon-trains, fell sick. He was able to reach the ranch on the Purgatory River, and died there of pneumonia, May 19th. Mary, his eldest daughter, was with him.

Bent County, Colorado, still bears his name.

Charlie Russell, the future artist, was then five years old. You might think that hearing these things about his Bent cousins would discourage Charlie's desire to go west, but it didn't.

Note well that none of the above killings were caused by Indians going into white man's country: it was always the whites who went into Indian country.

Someone should write a tragic novel about the Baldy Bents of Lost Souls River. A Gothic novel. It would take a Faulkner to write it.

(For most, though not all, of the above, see *Bent's Fort* by David Lavender. It contains an immense amount of information and is well indexed.)

William's youngest brother, Silas Bent—later Captain— was with Perry at the opening of Japan. This Captain Silas Bent was an important person in his own right, mapping the Japanese currents, especially the Kuro Shiwo, the Black Tide, which controls Japan's climate and corresponds to the Atlantic Gulf Stream. He too had dealt with Indians in the Seminole War. He resigned his Commission at the start of the Civil War but did not fight for the South.

The other side of the family had also dealt with Indians way back in colonial days. For example, when Charlie's elder brother, Silas Bent Russell, grew up, he married Anne Eliot Clendenin, a great granddaughter of Gloriana Austin, daughter of Moses Austin and sister of Stephen Austin who founded Texas. As recently as 1938, marauders from the Lone Star State stole by night into Potosi, Missouri, and tried to dig up Moses and move his bones to Texas; but the Missourians awoke just in time and chased the Longhorns home.

26

How Three Ancestors Got Scalped

This Anne Eliot Clendenin was also a direct descendant of John Eliot, "the Apostle to the Indians," who translated the Bible into Mohawk. When the Christian Colonists shipped their Indian captives down to Cuba to sell them into slavery—where the climate soon killed them in the sugar cane fields—only two men in the whole colony protested. One of them was John Eliot.

Charlie Russell was himself directly descended from the Hicks family of Hicksville and Hempstead, Long Island, from the Wolfert Eckers—whose house on the Hudson was burnt by the English in the Revolution—and from the Van Tassels who figure in *The Legend Of Sleepy Hollow*.

So much for ancestors.

~§ 4 §~

Boyhood Cultural Influences

Charlie's father, Charles Silas Russell—son of James Russell and Lucy Bent—was a healthy optimist who smoked cigars right down to the bitter tip, skewering the tip with a toothpick when it got too short and too hot to hold. He drank whiskey three times daily, and ate whatever he pleased as long as he lived. I remember, when he was old and lived with us, seeing him sit by the table in the livingroom and consume most of a box of candy while he was reading: and he devoured any kind of book with the same appetite and enjoyed just as much as the assembled offspring the boy's books he read aloud.

He also, when necessary, whipped the assembled offspring with a canvas-backed razor-strop without inducing any complexes, neuroses, or other modern improvements.

Charlie's mother, Mary Mead Russell—we have her picture, taken the year she married, and if it doesn't flatter her she was a beauty—was, after the fashion of the time, kept busy having babies—two died too young to be christened—but as she died when I was a child I don't remember much about her. Charles senior survived a full generation and married again.

Though not wealthy, the four families were comfortably off. In the Civil War they were Southern sympathizers but never owned any slaves. They had an immense tract of land in what is now South St. Louis, nine streets are still named after different members—a cousin, Anne Russell Allen, gave her name to three streets arranged in that order—and had they shown foresight, they should, with the steadily increasing demand for fireclay, have become rich, as the Evans and Howards and Christies and Walshes and other competitors did. But the Russells preferred to live right now and not worry about the future.

This preference was influenced by one of the uncles, Trumbull Gustine Russell. All the children were afraid of his eagle eye and his gray goatee and the important way he cleared his throat; he declared he couldn't live on chips and whetstones, so he lived on the company till. The others protested but joined him. For years they went along swimmingly, declaring a dividend every time they got a nice order and not setting up anything for depreciation or even for replacement and repairs. Why should they as long as the farm produced both coal and fireclay—the famous Cheltenham clay which made St. Louis known wherever men used firebrick?

But Uncle John played the organ and chewed tobacco. He had a small pipe-organ installed in the house and played it, preferably after midnight when the family had gone to bed, leaning over at intervals to spill tobacco juice back of the pipes. In the end he waterlogged the organ. When you pressed the foot pedal, the treble pipes gurgled, *oogle, oogle,* and gave a liquid note. All the family, what's left of them, deny this—they say Charlie invented it. However there certainly was an organ, and Uncle John did chew. It's only Indians who swallow tobacco juice; the white man has to spill.

When Charlie's brother Bent grew up and married and had a house of his own—he was a civil engineer and worked for the Water Department—he kept in the front hall an ornamental bronze turtle. You stepped on the head, the carapace rose up, and there was a spittoon. And yet people talk about the Middle West as if it was purely utilitarian and had no arts or artifacts of its own. Bent was my father, the turtle's name was *Ee-sop* and I used to play with him when mother wasn't looking. As civilization slowly overtook us, mother suppressed *Ee-sop*.

But all this, of course, came a generation later.

In Charlie's boyhood people did more visiting than they do now, whole families staying with their relatives for months, and though there was not much drunkenness the men drank whiskey every day just as the ladies drank coffee. (When they built the transcontinental railroad the contract stated that part of the men's pay would be in whiskey.)

Every country house had in front of it a circular bed of mint. Every sideboard had a brass or silver tray and on it two matched vessels with long necks and glass stoppers—a "caraff" for water and a decanter. (I don't know why they decanted the whiskey. Perhaps they were ashamed of the brand. Or maybe it hadn't paid taxes.) Every visitor was given a drink.

The whiskey in those days was fiery stuff. You'd throw half a glassful down your neck—without touching lips or tongue—and then, quick, before your liver burst into flames, grab for the water.

For five minutes after taking a drink nobody said anything—they couldn't. They just stood there and goggled at each other.

After a couple of drinks like that you could go out and really cope with the world. Some of the family did some high-grade coping—which is why we are now nearly extinct.

At least that's how Charlie told it afterward, but he may have exaggerated.

The kids, of course, got no whiskey, only in summertime an occasional mint julep—mostly cracked ice and sugar. Charlie could remember his first white sugar. Before that it was brown and juicy stuff which came in big hunks and had quite a different taste. It also had embedded in it enormous cockroaches—the American equivalent of flies in amber. Americans always do everything bigger: the classical fly in amber was small potatoes compared to the American roach.

Baseball does not seem to have been popular at Oak Hill. Rugby was unknown but they played a primitive kind of soccer, mostly a shin-kicking contest; the kid who could take it, and keep taking it, right on the shin, won the game. More often they played Settlers and Indians, cutting the sweat-band out of an old hat and sticking it full of feathers.

Also they hunted; crows, rabbits, squirrels, foxes— anything that ran or jumped or flew.

Between times they went around getting in trouble. My father Bent, for instance, Charlie's elder brother, the gadget engineer, was wandering through the "works" one Sunday morning and it occurred to him that he had never climbed down the mine chain in the shaft. Which he proceeded to do. He climbed down all right and after poking around in the dark and discovering that there was too much mysterious dripping in the sumps, and much too many echoes, he decided to climb up again; but couldn't. He'd get within ten feet of the top and then his arms would give out and he had to get down again, quick, or fall. He stayed down all day, accompanied by the echoes, and it wasn't till late afternoon that the yard boss, cutting across through the property, heard his yells and wound him up on the chain. Net result, broken blisters on his palms, the knees rubbed out of his Sunday pants, and an enthusiastic seance with the strop.

Public too, lest the smaller kids go and do likewise.

But they all learned to climb. Hay baling machines were new then, and Bent, fooling around the hay barn, climbed ten or twelve feet up the glossy yellow cliff of the stacked bales and then climbed down again, dusting his long and skinny hands as if he had really done something.

The smaller kids admired and prepared to imitate, but a fat and rather elderly riverside bum who was working on the farm for a few days, said, "Here's how to do it!" and jabbing toes and flat palms in between the bales he ran straight up the stack, right to the gable—and it was a high-pitched roof.

It looked easy the way he did it, just like a squirrel scampering up a tree, but when you tried you found that if you slowed up before you reached the top, or if your hand slipped, or your arms gave out, you slid, face-front, down the bales, polishing your nose the wrong way—and hay cuts like glass—and got a back-busting fall. A fall with sound effects from the younger brethren.

As soon as they were big enough to be trusted with a gun —or, as their mothers thought, much sooner—they began hunting. Bent, as the eldest, had a gun of his own, a muzzle-loader, but the small fry hunted in packs—one gun to a whole bunch of boys. They had strict orders to stay *back* of the gun.

Though the Americans had already exterminated the famous wild pigeons which once in their migrations darkened the sky and eclipsed the sun, there was still no closed season, no game was protected.

One of the boys' favorite songs was a rigamarole identifying the different species by their caudal appendages:

> The raccoon's tail has rings all around,
> The possum's tail hit drags the ground,
> The rabbit's tail hit is so short
> He has no tail a-tall.

But it was only on special occasions, and under grown-up guidance, that they went coon hunting with lanterns.

Mostly they shot birds, doves, blue jays, red headed woodpeckers—*any*thing that flew.

Crows were plentiful but just as cagey as they are now— hard to get within range and almost impossible to get a second shot at. You had to kill with the first.

One bright morning before breakfast Bent heard the whole flock down at the far end of the corn field, cawing and croaking and hollering, ganging a hawk they had cornered in a tree. Knowing he would get no second shot, Bent took only the charge in his gun, stalked them through the corn, and actually got within range. He winged the biggest and blackest and brought it down just at the edge of the corn but the crow was only wounded, fluttering and flapping and jumping and squawking to heaven, trying to fly with one wing. His brethren heard him and instead of taking flight the whole flock circled about the fallen leader, yelling and raising cain and acting as if they were going to knock Bent's eyes out. All his life he never forgot his regret that he hadn't brought along a second charge; he could have killed half a dozen.

Here is Charlie's description—written forty years after—of one of *his* hunts:

"——seeing these birds in these woods [i.e., the remnant of Grandma's Woods] reminds me of when I was a youngster of about 9 winters hunting with a party of kids. We had one gun   this weapon was the old time muzzel loading musket   there was but one boy in the party long enough to lode her without the aid of a stump   so of corse he packed the ammunition an done most of the loding. we were shooting in turns at aney thing in sight. well I kept belly-aking saying My turn   an the big kid saying Youl get yours   an I did. When he loded for me I remember how the rod jumped clear of the barel   [i.e., he rammed in so much powder]   He spent five or more miuntes tamping the lode   then handing the gun to me said Thair that would kill a Tiger   an I think it would if hed been on the same end I was.   My game was crows.   I climbed to the top of a rail fence to get cleane range.   and then as the Books say for an instant my hawk eye measured the glistening barrel   then the death like stillness was broken by the crack of my faithful wepon   an I kept it broken with howls for quite a while."

The quotation is from a letter illuminated in water-color—but almost devoid of punctuation—written to old Mr. Trigg of Great Falls when Charlie visited St. Louis in

1903. The drawing shows autumn woods, a bursting cloud of smoke, the dogs running away, the small boys crouching behind a tree, the big boy laughing, and Charlie being kicked backward off a high rail fence.

Charlie, who seems to have been his father's favorite, had a pony of his own named Gyp, but all the boys learned to ride. Like other country people they always had carriage horses, the farm required several work teams, at the "diggin's" they used both horses and mules; so there was plenty of horsekind for the kids to practice on.

Of course, the boys all had dogs, so many that it was a fixed rule, "no dogs allowed in the house." This was one of "the laws of the Meads and Russells that altereth not." I didn't realize till I went to school that this family saying was a twist from the Greek—the Laws of the Medes and Persians.

Charlie had a lot of Mead cousins—his mother was Mary Mead, the daughter of a St. Louis jeweler. Later, at the time of the St. Louis World Fair, 1904, an English Mead, an engineer, and his son stayed with the St. Louis Meads and had dinner at our house.

The Russells, of course, were not the only big landowners on the Diggins; the Binghams had a large "plantation" along Bingham Avenue, as did the Christy family and others. Here are some notes from outside the family record: They come from *The Old Gravois Coal Diggins* by Mary Joan Boyer.

"I have never read a word about a part of St. Louis which used to be known as the Old Gravois Coal Diggins. Yet my parents told me that it was the Diggins that enticed my Scotch grandfather, who had located in Albany, on his arrival from Scotland, and my English grandfather, who had located in Cleveland, to Missouri. Both grandfathers hoped to get rich at coal mining. In addition to coal on the

34

Diggins, there was fireclay. And a few miles south of St. Louis there was lead. [It was from Missouri lead mines that Moses and Stephen Austin got the money for their Texas adventure.]

"The Gravois Diggins were marked all over with coal pits and pit banks—the refuse from the coal pits—and sink holes where pits had been. [When they abandon a mine they "pull the props" and the overload settles.] Morganford Road ran through one of the old pit banks near the location of the German Lutheran Church at Meramac Street.

"The first Oak Hill School on the Diggins was on Russell property opposite the Company Store on Morganford Road. The second Oak Hill school was on Tholozan Avenue near Holy Innocents Church, which, according to old records, was built as a memorial to a daughter of the Parkers. The second school had two rooms, one downstairs, the other up.

"There were two grocery stores and two saloons on the Diggins. One store was kept by a widow named Woodruff—her son John became manager of the Company Store with his brother William as assistant.

"The other store, and saloon combined, was kept by a German named Beck, a long low-built place with a porch all across the front. As Beck's business grew he added more rooms to the place.——he became owner of a large part of the Diggins. He built a big brick building on the corner of Beck Avenue and Morganford Road, had himself made postmaster, and changed the name of the Gravois Coal Diggins to Beckville.   .

"The other saloon on the Diggins was run by a cripple named Wandless——.

"The first and only drygoods store on the Diggins in early days was owned by a Latter-Days Saints minister [Mormon] named Hazeldine——.

"Before the Civil War liberated the slaves, each plantation had its own blacksmith. After the war a man named Grimm started the first blacksmith shop on the Diggins.

"Then there was Shinbiddle's place on the edge of the Diggins opposite the spot now occupied by the Bevo Mill—.

"Bamberger's Grove—where the House of the Good Shepherd now stands—was laid out like a park with gravel paths, flower beds, and here and there an iron deer, life-size, half hidden in the shrubbery. There was a pavilion for dancing, seats and tables and, of course, a bar.——later a hall was built there——Lodge meetings were held in the room upstairs and dances below. The women and girls wore calico dresses for the dances——."

Old Johnny Woodruff, who, when I knew him, kept the stock books at the Oak Hill plant, told me he started work, at twelve, as a plough boy on the Russell farm, and so did Bill Gutgeschell, the factory foreman. Bert Morris, the Superintendent, also began at twelve years old by off-bearing handmade brick on a wooden pallet.

(You off-bear brick on a pallet—each brick seven and a half pounds—for a ten-hour day and you'll earn your living. In the evening after supper the other boys played ball and tag in the street, but Bert just sat on the front steps; he was too tired to play.)

When I knew them they were all elderly, and all had worked all their lives for the Company.

Woodruff remembered Charlie as a wild, crazy kind of kid who never said much but was always very active.

Charlie's boyhood was only three generations ago: How did he think? Much as small boys do now but with this difference—there were almost no gadgets.

For instance, there were no elevators: if you lived, or worked on the sixth floor you climbed six flights of steps.

Gas lighting was new then. There were no electric lights, not even arc-lights, no flashlights, no telephones. No movies, no radio, no television. The explosive engine had not been invented, so there were no flying machines except the gas balloon of the County Fair and the paper hot-air balloon of the Fourth of July. There were no autos, no trucks, no motor buses, no speedboats. Because there were no motors, gasoline was so worthless that they poured it down the sewer.

The Parker-Russell M. & M. Co. designed, manufactured, erected and put in operation coal gas benches for gas-plants. One problem was, what to do with the tar? Tar was used for roofing and caulking and that's about all. There were no tar products, no plastics, not even celluloid, no synthetic flavors, no aspirin, and no vitamins. There was no major league ball, no professional football or hockey, no spectator sports of any kind except boxing, wrestling, cock-fighting, horse races and horse shows. The County Fair and the State Fair were the big events of the year. In St. Louis *the* big event was the Veiled Prophet's Parade.

There was very little imported food. At Christmas each child got one orange. It looked like an orange—it wasn't dyed.

Most men chewed tobacco—in the Ozarks both men and women chewed snuff—but nobody chewed gum: there wasn't any. And no ice cream.

To offset all this there was still a Frontier. It played an enormous part in Charlie's thought. Even as a child he couldn't help knowing that the thousands of strangers pouring through St. Louis were all of them heading west.

At Oak Hill when Charlie climbed out a top window onto the roof to look at the sunset, he was looking at the Frontier. St. Louis, on the west bank of the Mississippi, was the jumping-off place: right there the West began. During its short life, the Pony Express started from the other edge of the state at Rubidoux Landing.

Of course, Charlie as a child did not put all this stuff into words. Even as a man he didn't put such stuff into words: he put it into pictures.

But the climax and catastrophe of Charlie's boyhood was the great conspiracy to gang the teacher.

The big boys got it up, the tough kids from the Diggins —Bent and the elder cousins being then old enough to go to school in St. Louis—but Charlie, young, small, bold, and inexperienced, was the one who took the plot most seriously. *He* really meant it. It was agreed that the next time the teacher started to whip the biggest boy the whole school would rise in fury.

When the great hour came the school *did* rise—but only to see the better. Charlie alone started forward, a small blonde bulldog (being one of the littlest he sat in the front row) and got what he should have expected.

As he expressed it, right from the jump it was the teacher's fight—the first round closed with Charlie bottom up and on the receiving end of the biggest whipping the school had ever seen.

"*Now* go home and tell your mother!" said teacher.

Charlie did—he really should have known better—mother told father and after supper Charlie received again. Moreover he took back with him next morning an open letter telling the teacher to go as far as he liked.

It all came under the head of education—after this no more conspiring. On the rare occasions when Charlie had to fight he did it on his own. He never did much fighting; he made friends too easily, and he wasn't the type that people pick on—very much not that type.

(Twenty years later, visiting the family in St. Louis, Charlie rode one evening on the back platform of the street car, and all the way uptown a drunk, a total stranger, insisted on talking to him, the stupid, noisy, repetitious talk of the tiresome souse. To which Charlie listened very patiently, laughing at jokes with no laugh in them and answering yes and no. Finally a second drunk—hitherto silent and also a stranger—leaned over and tapped Charlie's shoulder and said earnestly, "Mister, if I was as hard looking as you are, I wouldn't let *any*body talk to me!")

Going to school in the city, Bent had to rise early, and it was his habit to wake Charlie by jerking off the blankets and chanting, "Arouse, Jove, and slay thy meat!"

Which Charlie supposed was a quotation from Homer or something.

Long after I repeated this to Bent (my father). He denied it flatly, couldn't remember any such quotation; and I am sure that even as a boy he would never have said "Arouse."

So here you have two brothers—both honest as men go—contradicting each other. Did Bent really say something of the kind and then forget it utterly, or did Charlie's unconscious just invent the whole thing and attribute it to his big brother?

Perhaps it was a tribal or racial memory, a dim echo of something that happened in a former life, a preview Bent waking a preview brother long before Charlie was Charlie.

⚜ 5 ⚜

Early Art Influences

As the children grew older, the four families generally wintered in St. Louis. Bent and most of the others had been born at Oak Hill but Charlie was born in the city on the corner of 16th and Olive. In the course of time the house was torn down but after Charlie's death the Junior Chamber of Commerce set up a bronze marker. Bronze can be melted and sold over again, so the marker was stolen—*sic semper gloria* in the Middle West.

St. Louis was then the largest fur center in the world. Except for the new art museum there was not much art there, but on the steep east edge of town where the streets sloped down to the levee with its endless row of paddle-wheel steamers, was the old St. Louis Court House, where, before the Civil War, they sold slaves at public auction, standing them up on a block to be fingered and felt over; and this Court House had—and still has—richly colored murals by Carl Wimar, the first St. Louis artist. Wimar ran to gorgeous red sunsets and silvery moonlit rivers, and the new Art Museum had several of his paintings—*A Buffalo Hunt, Indians Approaching A Trading Post,* and *The Captive Charger.*

They were really good work and Charlie admired them intensely though he remarked that the excessively woolly buffalos had no necks and couldn't graze unless they got down flat, like an alligator. He liked especially *The Captive Charger,* Indians leading off a cavalry horse with sabre

40

still slung from saddle. Later, when he had lived among the Indians, Charlie realized that the Indian wouldn't be *leading* the horse—he'd ride it.

The Museum must have been quite small and I don't know where it was located in Charlie's boyhood, but a generation later, when I went to school at 19th and Washington, it was only a couple of blocks off and we kids used to infest it on Free Day. One enterprising youth discovered that on certain classical bronzes the fig leaves—evidently an afterthought—were hinged and could be propped up with a match. We left them propped—like an awning—and the guards ran us out.

At this same boys' school, at that same time, was the now famous T. S. Eliot. Though he early shook the Middle West off his shoes and went to England, he was never able to shake it out of his blood and it bore fruit in *The Waste Land* (Westland?). It looks as if the richer the country from which he comes, the more pessimistic the writer. Compare Mark Twain. But this has nothing to do with Charlie. Unless indeed you explain it by saying that Charlie went west and stayed hopeful, whereas Eliot, Mark Twain, Ambrose Bierce and the rest went east, saw Europe, and were embittered for life. It is possible that Europeans might reject this explanation.

Psuedo-classical bronzes did not interest Charlie, but his last winter in St. Louis he was sent to art school. Where he was set to drawing still life models, cones and cubes and so forth—which wasn't at all what he wanted to draw. He went only twice, then he began playing hookey—just as he did from regular school—and spent his days on the levee, admiring the river men and trappers and fur traders, and watching them load the trade-boats—wood-burners—that crawled slowly up the Mississippi to Columbia Bottoms and then up the snag-filled Missouri to Fort Benton in the far-off and immense Montana Territory. Which Charlie imagined as an endless Mayne Reid prairie, covered, like the Kansas prairie, with waist-deep grass through which galloped herds of buffalo hunted by Indians—in war-bonnets—and the Indians hunted by blueclad, yellow-striped cavalry. He had no idea how the Montana prairie really looked with sage and bunch-grass and in the background flat-topped buttes and fantastic bad-lands.

Those were the days of the last Indian Wars when the U.S. generals—hardened to massacre by the march through Georgia—deliberately provoked the plains tribes into revolt and then butchered them at Wounded Knee and other places of slaughter. The Indians, of course, had no chance against disciplined soldiers. It wasn't the red man's skill but the white man's recklessness that caused the Custer massacre on the Little Big Horn.

Charlie's great-uncle, William Bent of Bent's Fort— though two of his halfbreed sons were in the Southern army— played a great part in keeping the Indians out of the Civil War. When the chiefs came to him for advice he told them to lay low, stay on their own range and keep clear of the ruckus. And keep their young men home; among the tribes it was always the young men who made trouble.

Boys, too, make trouble. As Charlie grew bigger, he got harder to control, and in his early teens—but they didn't talk about teen-agers then—he and his friend Archie Douglas played hookey for nearly two months before they got caught. Finally they ran away from home.

Having very little money they started early and set out afoot across Missouri, getting lifts on farm wagons and intending to work their way to Montana Territory. By night they were in parts quite new to them and stopped at a farmhouse and asked for work. The farmer sized them up and fed them and gave them work—plenty of it—and after a couple of days Archie weakened—or perhaps he was just more intelligent—and went home. Charlie, more resolute, stuck it out for weeks, and when at last he returned to Oak Hill, the family acted as if he hadn't been away. His father had heard from the farmer and knew all the time where he was.

Foreseeing that Charlie would certainly run away again, Charles Senior sent him to military school at Burlington, New Jersey. Military school was the place you sent boys you couldn't control at home. The school might or might not impart an education but it did control. The tougher the kid, the tougher the treatment.

Charlie, not bad but in his own way intractable, spent hours walking guard—the regulation penalty for inattention —and was cured, permanently, of any ambition to be a soldier.

Finding he couldn't buck the faculty, he got his classwork done, especially arithmetic, by getting other boys to do it for him, bribing them with little figures of Indians and animals and caricatures of the teacher in unedifying poses. Logical result: confiscation of the art, its secret exhibition at instructors' mess, and, for the artist, more guard duty.

Under this system Charlie's mouth got more stubborn still and his eyes fiercer, but he learned some of the hard facts of life and came home determined not to go back to school.

His father saw and made the big decision and took the big risk. Said he, "Charles, how would you like to go West? A friend of mine, Mr. Pike Miller, has a sheep ranch out in the Montana Territory and is willing to teach you the business. Remember, you'll be a long ways from home—much further than you were at school! But perhaps a few weeks' real hardship will make you more ready to get an education."

So early in March, 1880, just before his sixteenth birthday, Charlie went west.

He was not the first of the family to go there. His great uncle, George Bent, elder brother of William Bent of Bent's Fort, was fur-trading on the Upper Missouri in what is now Montana as early as 1816.

Charlie Russell Meets His Totem

Pike Miller had a ranch in the Judith Basin and ran sheep on the Upper Judith River in central Montana. Instead of taking a steamboat up the Missouri, as Charlie had always expected, he and Pike went by way of the Utah Northern Railroad to Red Rock, and thence by stagecoach overland to Last Chance Gulch, or, as they now call it, Helena, the largest town in the whole Montana Territory.

It was from a train window that Charlie got his first look at the great plains and saw the mountains come up over the edge—real mountains such as he had never seen: mountains with snow on them.

But it was from the driver's seat of the stagecoach that he began to see things in close detail—a troop of booted cavalry, blueclad, with Civil War sabres; a coyote watching them from up on a benchland; and a bunch of pronghorns (antelope) skimming away, like dust, in the distance.

At the top of a rise the stage stopped to blow the horses, and the passengers got down to stretch their legs; and there, back from the road and under a clump of bunch-grass, Charlie found his first buffalo skull, bleached chalk white and with the nose bones split but the horns still on. Of course, he had seen cow skulls in Missouri but they were not magic like this.

You figure him as a sturdy tow-headed kid in city clothes—but he had already got rid of his necktie—as unsentimental looking a person as it is possible to imagine—considering the skull and its deep eye-sockets, turning it over with his foot, and stooping and rubbing it with his thumb to see if the white came off. He didn't make any poor Yorick oration.

The early Greeks saved the skulls of the sacrificial cattle and boiled them clean and nailed them up on the walls of their wooden temples. Where they were so impressive with their dark eye sockets—the emptiness and utterness of death—that when the Greeks learned to build in stone they carved the skulls in marble hung with garlands; and architects have been using them ever since—mostly all out of proportion.

Charlie knew little and cared less about the early Greeks, but afterward when he became an artist he took the buffalo skull for his trademark. The Bull's Head, he called it.

At the time he thought little about it—there was too much to see. Much that you can't see now.

Montana did not look as it does today. The gang-plow had not yet broken the prairie sod, packed hard and thick for thousands of years by the migrating buffalo. There were no fences, no wheat, no sugar beets, no rutabagas; no dandelions along the right of way; no trees except willows and cottonwoods along the river. No tumbleweed—that modern substitute for the stampeding buffalo—rolling across the open before the wind.(The tumbleweed came in with the first wheat.) No English sparrows—brought to America, like the English dandelion, because they were so cute.

There were no foreigners, almost no Negroes, but plenty of French Canadians, mostly halfbreeds. Besides the tribes already rounded up and herded on reservations, there were still quite a few Indians on the loose. Except for squaws and prostitutes there were very few women. Like

Canada geese, prostitutes migrated with the seasons. In spring, boatloads of girls came up the Missouri to Fort Benton to summer in Montana; and in fall went back down river to winter in St. Louis. Some didn't go back—they got married.

Except small local herds, there were no cattle. The first Texas longhorns were driven north to Montana two years after Charlie got there. Not shipped in cattle-cars but trail-driven overland across the unfenced prairie, fording creeks and swimming rivers, and being months on the way.

Helena with its mountain right behind it was a revelation to Charlie—a long street of plank shacks, mostly one-story but some with false fronts to suggest a second floor, wooden sidewalks, already in bad shape, and a dirt street always either rolling with dust or kneedeep in mud except when it was frozen hard in winter. Every fourth or fifth house was a saloon. Almost everybody wore a belt and a gun; some wore two.

The street was lined with freight outfits, two or three huge covered wagons chained end to end and drawn by twelve or even fourteen span of horses or, sometimes, by the famous Missouri mules. The nigh-wheeler—next to the front wagon—was saddled. The jerk-line man rode him, jerking the line that led to the lead span. Beside the jerk-line man there were bull-whackers and mule-skinners snapping whips with sixteen-foot lashes that popped like a rifle report. They boasted they could snap a horsefly off the leader's eyelashes without making him wink. They could also lay a mule's back open with one cut. The skinner's talk was as hide-blistering as his whip. and the team, especially the mules, understood profanity and answered in kind with snorts and squeals and bawls of defiance, kicking and biting like stallions. And a mule can bite like a bear-trap and kick with both ends.

Books always talk about range horses, and cattle, and sheep, but the Missouri mule played as big a part as the horse in settling the West.

It was a U.S. cavalry general who described the army pack-mule:—

> The aw-ee-ing,
> Kicking, jawing,
> Bucking, biting,
> Swearing, fighting,
> Rat-tailed, piebald,
> Glistening eye-balled,
> Missouri army mule.

And, of course, besides mule teams and horse teams, there were bull-teams—really oxen, not bulls—as slow as the grace of God. In the southwestern deserts the U.S. army even tried camels but the packers didn't like the ugly, grunting, stubborn, spitting beasts and didn't give them a fair trial. The British army used thousands of camels. But there were no camels in Helena.

Charlie, not saying much and secretly a bit cowed, looked the confusion over and knew, without needing to say so, that this was his country; here was where he belonged. He knew right then that he was going to stay. And he was going to get clothes to suit the country.

Especially when he saw a whole family of French Canuck halfbreeds ride single file down the street, dressed more or less like Indians, with moccasins, sashes, and blanket *capotes*—a sort of bathrobe overcoat made of a white Hudson Bay blanket with three or four red bands at the edge to show the thickness of the weave—but wearing broad-brimmed hats and each with a covered rifle across in front of him.

There were Indians too—it was ration time for the red men—standing around on the edge of the confusion or riding through it in their quiet way, all wearing skin leggings and robes. Buffalo robes, mostly, stripped of hair and chewed soft by the squaws.

The Indian woman made arrows the same way: held one end in her teeth and twirled the shaft between her palms to break the pith inside. If you don't break the pith it will dry crooked and warp the shaft. Want to be sure it's a real Indian arrow? Look for the tooth marks on it, the lady's bite.

The Indians on their pinto ponies, riding through Helena to get the government ration, said even less than Charlie. Indeed said nothing except an occasional long-drawn "Ho-ho-*hay*-eeeee!" The Ho-ho, deep and guttural; the *hay* expressing surprise.

They were surprised at the white man's ways—who wouldn't be?

Long afterwards, when I knew him, Charlie declared that in his whole life he had never heard an Indian say "Ugh! Ugh!" as they do in two-gun westerns and the movies.

Teddy Roosevelt, that greatest, or at least most vociferous, of all westerners, once made a long oration to the Indians, and whenever he paused for breath and applause, the assembled braves, squatting on their hunkers, would put a cupped hand up across their lips and utter a deep-mouthed "Bush-*wah*!"

As the speech went on and on, it became a regular chorus, "Bush-*wah!* Bush-*wah!*"

Teddy asked the Government Agent what Bush-wah meant.

The Agent blushed and fidgetted and looked uncomfortable and answered in a whisper, "I'm afraid it means buffalo chips."

Buffalo chips—otherwise cow-flops—are what you burn out on the prairie where there isn't any wood. You prop up three on edge like cards—they're flat as a pancake—and they burn with a bright blue flame and a strong smell of ammonia. After months of cooking over a chip fire you get so used to the ammonia flavor that home cooking seems sort of tasteless.

They outfitted in Helena, Pike buying a wagon and four horses, and Charlie paying for two of them. These were not Indian ponies but big work horses and one of Charlie's was a mare.

Charlie also bought a buckskin shirt and a big hat with a fancy band on it and a Hudson Bay sash, nine foot long and colored red, blue, yellow, green, and purple—which Pike considered damn foolishness.

But Charlie just shut his mouth—hard—and went ahead and bought 'em: yes, and wore 'em. That's how he got his first nickname—Buckskin Kid.

Loading up with grub, they pulled out for Judith Gap, the pass into the Basin. There was no road, only a very rough wagon trail, and they had a hard time crossing the Crazy Mountains, where one of their horses gave out.

They finally got across but Charlie was off wagon travel for life. Thenceforth he stuck to pack and saddle horses, which can go almost anywhere that a man can go.

He was soon off the sheep too. The shepherd is a romantic figure in poetry, but in Montana, ah how different! In India they have a brain-fever bird which in the hot weather repeats one note over and over until the white man goes crazy. You listen to a herd of sheep, *blat, blat, blat, blat, blat,* for twenty-four hours and you won't need any brain-fever bird. And you can't get away from it—you can hear it for miles. And they're such nasty, dirty looking beasts. Wherever they go they leave a desert; they graze the grass down to the roots.

Charlie, who always knew what he didn't like, stood it a few weeks, and then he and Pike had an argument and split up, and Charlie took his two horses and quit the ranch. The ranchers didn't act as if they were going to miss him very much, as Pike and everybody around there considered the Russell kid pretty ornery. By which they probably meant that he was stubborn and wouldn't let them boss him.

Charlie knew that a stage station down the valley needed a stock-herder, but when he asked for the job he found that his eloquent explanation of just what he thought about sheep and sheep-herders, had got there ahead of him, and they were afraid to trust him with their horses: they thought he didn't like animals.

This was a blow he hadn't expected. He had no food and mighty little money, and no place to go, and no friends or even acquaintances except at the Miller ranch. And home and St. Louis were a long ways off.

Too proud and still too ignorant of western ways to say he was hungry—if he had they would certainly have fed him and staked him to some grub—he set out for the Judith River, leading his pack horse loaded with nothing except a very light bed. Bed-roll the westerners called it—a blanket or two rolled up inside a tarpy or a slicker.

By then it was late afternoon.

Of course, this wasn't much of an adventure compared to what he had read in Mayne Reid and *Frank on the Prairie* and other boys' books, but still, when you're sixteen and have never been alone before, it's kind of scary to see the shadows lengthen and blue dusk come oozing down the coulies, and not a sign of a ranch or a road or town, or anything except the empty open. And over there, in plain sight and still lit by the sun—which no longer lit the prairie—were the Crazies, so-called because of their queer, unnatural-looking peaks. They *do* look crazy and desolate. Indians call them the Ghost Mountains. Do you know what the sign-language word is for ghost? Big-Eyes-At-Night.

Charlie didn't believe in ghosts, but all the same he wasn't a bit comfortable.

Just at dark he came to the river and picketed his horses and made camp—which is to say built a fire and unrolled his bed.

He didn't enjoy the prospect of lying down and not knowing what was sneaking up on him, and running water—noiseless by day—does a lot of whispering and conspiring at night, and every little while it gives a nasty sort of chuckle as if to say, "In just a few minutes we'll grab him!"

Suddenly out of the darkness a harsh voice said, "Well, kid, what you doing here?"

Charlie almost jumped out of his pants and turned and saw a stranger sizing him up.

"Camping," said Charlie.

"Where's your grub?"

"Haven't got any."

"Where you going?"

"To get a job."

"Where you from?"

Charlie told him, and the stranger said, "You better come over and camp with me. I've got a lot of elk meat and beans and coffee. My name's Jake Hoover."

So Charlie threw in with him for the night and learned that Jake was a hunter and trapper—a meat-hunter—selling meat to the settlers and sending pelts and skins to the big trading post at Fort Benton. His way of life so suited the boy that they became partners and worked together two years.

Jake told Charlie to get rid of his big team horses, especially the mare, saying, "This is no place for a lady hoss —if she gets the notion she'll quit the country and take every cayuse in the basin with her."

Which in fact is how the plains Indians first got their horses—strays from the Spanish herds way down in Mexico.

And strays are nearly always led, at first, by a mare. Later one of her colts, a stallion, takes the lead and bosses his harem around.

It's remarkable how in only two centuries the plains Indians—who had never domesticated any animal except the dog—all got horses. And the same thing happened in lower South America, where the pampas tribes—who had always gone afoot—became a race of horsemen.

The horse changed the Indian's whole way of life and began a new culture. Tribes which had farmed stopped farming and took to hunting on horseback. Riding horses is much more interesting than cutting sprouts—also easier.

It was a real culture: a civilization complete in itself, self-sufficient and self-sustaining. But for the white man's coming it could have gone on indefinitely, slowly complicating and perfecting itself. It might have produced conquerors. Do you know that the three greatest conquerors were all nomads—and all *colored?* Attila the Hun, Genghis Khan the Mongol, Timur the Tartar, all conquered more widely than Alexander or Napoleon or the other white conquerors. But the Indians came late: the white man's superior weapons and superior numbers—not his superior courage—would say kaput to the red man.

Of course, horses on the loose increase quite rapidly. On the prairie they have no enemy except the wolf—and *he* can't do much unless he catches a horse bogged down in mud or snow. The mare has a colt every year till she's eighteen or twenty, and just a couple of hours after birth the colt can run almost as fast as his mother. In other ways, too, the mare is well able to take care of herself. In the hardest blizzard, when the prairie is glazed with ice, she can paw through it and get at the grass beneath.

Come to think of it, the Indian pony has as good a pedigree as any thoroughbred. When, set in motion by Mohammed, the Arabs out of Asia, conquered Egypt, they brought their horses with them to the Nile. Thence they spread west across the whole width of Africa, conquering the Moors; and the Moors in turn crossed the Strait of Gibraltar and conquered Spain, and brought their Arab horses with them. The modern Spaniards inherited both a lot of Moorish blood and Moorish horses and took them to the Americas where they became in time the Indian pony. First cousin, though he doesn't know it, to the race horse. For it was from the Godolphin Arabian, brought from Arabia to England, that all the modern thoroughbreds descend.

Charlie, though as stubborn as a blue mule, knew good advice when he got it. In just a few days they met a bunch of Pay-gan Indians—that's the tribal name; it doesn't mean pagan or heathen, though these were both.

This was Charlie's first encounter with the red men. He couldn't talk to them at all but Jake could—mostly in sign language—and they traded the two big work-horses for two smaller but more serviceable Indian ponies. One of them was a pinto (pinto means "painted") spotted white and bay and brown with black legs and mane and tail. Charlie named him "Monte" after the Mexican card game. When they thus met, Charlie and Monte were both young; when Monte died of old age in 1904, Charlie had ridden and packed him thousands of miles. Everybody who knew Kid Russell knew Monte.

A water color dated 1905 and called "When I was a kid," shows Charlie and Monte crossing the mountains: Monte walking daintily downhill among sloping boulders, picking his way; and Charlie—being a kid—looking as fierce as possible in a beaded buckskin shirt and leggings, with a big sheath-knife in his sash, and a covered Winchester across the horn in front of him. He is smoking a cigaret and looking tough—exactly the same expression that you can see today on the corner hep-cats, punks and so forth in L.A. or New York. Behind him, winding single-file among the rocks, come the pack horses, and behind them—up on the sky-line—Jake Hoover, not looking tough, just looking what he was—a mountain-man on his way to a good time in town.

Jake and Charlie had six horses—a saddle horse apiece and four packs. They hunted and trapped, selling bear, deer, and elk-meat to the settlers who were trickling into the country, and sending furs and skins to the big trading post at Fort Benton on the Upper Missouri. An ideal life for Charlie.

Later, when he began whoring around and drinking and gambling he had, perhaps, more fun—or at least more noisy fun—but never again the perfection of that first year in the foothills, up in the mountains, and out on the plains. Never again the thrill when for the first time he and Jake and the packs went clattering into town. You're young only once. Charlie was young the right way—and look what it did for him.

When he was old and tired, he always said that no matter what happened, "I'm glad I lived when I did—not twenty years later. I saw things when they were new."

Of course, he was new too then, he and Monte. And Jake, though he seemed old, or at least elderly, was really only thirty.

It's new eyes that make a new world.

Jake had a log cabin and what he called a ranch up in the edge of the foothills and was so far civilized that he kept a few hens and a rooster. The latter, having no competition and supposing himself the only rooster in the universe, got very cocky and bossed the hens around and even talked tough to Jake.

Once when Jake was in town raising hell, Charlie came back to the ranch to feed the stock and stayed there alone several days and amused himself by making passes at the rooster every time he entered the corral; but he was careful always to give the rooster the fight, that is to run away and leave him in possession of the field. The rooster began to think himself invincible.

Jake came home at last, broke and a bit shaky from his diversions, and shed his boots and went out, barefoot, with a frying-pan full of scraps to feed the chickens. The hens knew him and came cluttering about his feet to get their rations but the rooster, swollen up like a turkey-cock with self-importance, stayed aloof for the moment, working up a swell rage and enjoying it. Then, just as Jake stooped over to talk to the hens, the rooster ran up behind and jumped him and jabbed both spurs into Jake's bare ankle. It hurt. It also surprised Jake, who wasn't expecting to be jumped in his own corral. And when he turned, the rooster flew at his face. Jake was in no mood to give away a fight. He hit out with the frying-pan and killed the rooster dead.

"A hell of a rancher you are!" said Charlie. "*Now* what are the hens going to do?"

"I guess they'll do without," said Jake. "God damn his guts—trying to crawl my hump in my own corral! I must be in awful shape when even the roosters pick on me!"

For Jake and Charlie were both innocent enough to suppose that to lay eggs the hens need a rooster around.

The next time Jake was in town Charlie had a much more scary adventure.

Long before the sun clears the horizon there is plenty of light to travel by. Charlie was in the cabin starting breakfast, and just at sun-up he heard hoofs outside—not iron horseshoes but a barefoot pony. He stepped to the door, and there, swinging down from saddle, was a blanket Indian, a big fierce-looking buck with his hair combed all on one side and a hawk feather in it at a raking angle, and in his free hand a rifle.

Charlie's heart jumped and went into reverse. It made his blood flow backward just to look at him.

Charlie Russell Meets His Totem

The buck didn't hobble or tie his horse; he just dropped the end of the long line on the ground. (Indians used neither bit nor headstall; they rode with only one rein, a rawhide rope tied around the pony's lower jaw. The pony soon got bridlewise and divined what his rider wanted; he didn't wait to have his jaw jerked sideways.)

"How!" said the buck, and he crooked the rifle in the bend of his arm and strode up to the door—Charlie making way for him—and stalked in.

It was peace time, no war was going on, but the Indians had a lot to avenge: there were still plenty of white men who, whenever they caught an Indian alone, killed him just as a matter of course, and the Indians knew it, and, when they got the chance, did likewise. So Charlie had good reason to be scared.

He was just starting breakfast for one, and now he got breakfast for two.

When I was a boy I had for years a pen-and-ink sketch on brown wrapping paper—remember the old-fashioned butcher paper with black spots on it?—which Charlie sent home in a letter—Charlie, with his hair on end, tossing flapjacks and burning bacon, and the Indian with the rifle across his knees, sitting there watching him. The caption: "Plenty good breakfast."

In the end the Indian said "How!" again and departed, not lifting any scalps. Probably he had thought the whole thing funny, but Charlie hadn't. Much wit and humor depend on who's holding the gun.

⋐ 7 ⋑

Eleven Years Of Riding The Range

In the spring of '81 Charlie's father sent him the money to come home. Charlie returned it, saying he was going to save up enough to pay his own way; and the next spring he did go back to St. Louis. Charlie was now eighteen.

The family were surprised to see how he had changed and grown up, and what a good story-teller he had become, but were shocked at the way his English had deteriorated—full not merely of westernisms but plain bad grammar. His spelling, always a minus quantity, was now minus minimus. And they certainly didn't approve of his clothes. Especially his mother, his sister Sue, and his innumerable aunts and female cousins. But his boy cousins and his own brothers were fascinated: so much so that as soon as they finished school, both Bent and Ed went west, one to California, the other to Nevada and Montana.

The neighbors and family friends, though amused, were quite sure that Charlie Russell would never amount to much. "A cowboy," they pointed out, "is just a farmhand. He'll end up marrying a squaw."

The Russells were living in town and almost the first thing Charlie did was to take the train out to Oak Hill and visit his friends from the "diggin's."

He had promised his mother to be home for supper. Returning at twilight to the little wooden waiting-room on the Oak Hill branch of the Missouri Pacific, he saw a salesman, showily dressed, walking up and down the platform.

58

The salesman took one look at Charlie and immediately went around the corner of the station, ostensibly to get out of the wind and light a cigar. When he returned, rings, watch-chain, stick-pin, gold fraternity emblem—every article of jewelry—had disappeared. That's what *he* thought about Charlie; no wonder his mother didn't like Charlie's clothes. But Charlie just thought it funny.

Civilization made Charlie restless. He stayed home only four weeks and then returned to Montana, taking along his cousin Jim Fulkerson. At Billings Jim got mountain fever and the doctor made up a poultice so virulent in its action that when he applied it to the sick boy's face it burned his eyes and blinded him; it was a merciful thing when Jim died.

Paying the doctor had used up all their money. Alone again and afoot with only four bits in his pocket and two hundred miles between him and Hoover, things looked pretty bad. But Charlie met a fellow he knew and borrowed a horse and saddle and set out across country for the Judith.

It was early April and there were still patches of snow. Fifteen miles out of town he saw a string of riders coming to meet him. It was a cow outfit coming in to get a thousand dogies for the 12 Z & V outfit up in the Basin. (*Dough*-geez, please, to rhyme with dough, and it means ordinary range cattle.)

Charlie asked for a job, and the boss, John Cabler, hired him to night-wrangle the horses, that is, keep them together while the rest of the men were asleep around the chuck wagon. This night work was Charlie's first job as a puncher.

In those days most punchers owned a horse but did not use it when working, as the outfit provided each rider with a string of six or more horses—often even ten horses to each man, so even a small camp would have quite a herd.

Charlie, as Indian-faced as possible but privately not at all sure what was going to happen, ate an early and anxious supper, saddled up, and rode out to take charge.

"Whatever happens," said Cabler, "keep 'em together—don't let 'em squander out all over the flat."

Range horses sleep the first part of the night, but along about one o'clock in the morning they get up and graze for a couple of hours, and then lie down again. Never standing in stall, they haven't got the habit—like stable horses—of sleeping standing up.

Unlike the woods—which are as black as the inside of your hat, there's always some light on the prairie, even on a starless night; but in wet weather the night-wrangler has to see that the horses don't drift off across country in the rain; and there's always the danger that they, like cattle, may be stampeded by a thunder storm. The wrangler, riding slowly around the bunch, sings to himself not only because he's lonely but to warn the horses where he is so that they won't be startled when he suddenly looms up over them. One frightened horse, snorting and floundering up on his feet, can start the whole herd. The wrangler likewise wears his yellow slicker both because it keeps him warm—the high prairie, three thousand feet or more above sea level, gets cold at night—and also because it shows up in the dark and the horses can see it.

All of which Charlie knew by hearsay and now proved by experience. There was no storm that night and he held the bunch and was glad to see the dawn. Night-herding, sun-down to sun-up, is a long shift.

They were a month on the trail, and turned loose at Ross Fork, where they met the Judith Roundup.

They were getting back toward Hoover and the country Charlie knew, but he liked what he'd seen of the cow business and wanted more.

The round-up foreman, Horace Brewster, had just quarreled with his night herder and fired him; and Cabler gave Charlie such a good "recommend" that he got the job. He might not have got it if anybody there had known who he was—that's the kind of reputation his break with Pike Miller and his life with Jake Hoover had given him. Even as it was there were some doubts about him.

Old man True asked who the new night herder was, and Ed Older spoke up and said, "*I* think it's Kid Russell."

"Who's Kid Russell?"

"Why,"said Ed, "he's the kid who drew S. S. Hobson's ranch so real."

"Well,"says True, "if it's Buckskin Kid, I'm betting that by morning we'll be afoot!"

He didn't mean Charlie would steal the horses but just sleep on the job and let them get away. In dry weather the wrangler who wants to take a nap will find some horse on the edge of the herd and kick him up—make him move over— and then the wrangler lies down on the ground the horse has got warm.

But Charlie didn't sleep.

Though everybody called him "that ornery Kid Russell" he held the bunch, and at that time they had about four hundred saddle horses. And it wasn't so easy to keep an eye at night on four hundred horses in a country where there wasn't a fence between old Mexico and the Canadian line. This, you remember, was 1882, and Charlie was eighteen.

Charlie stayed with the outfit all summer, and next fall old man True hired him to night-herd beef, and for the best part of the next eleven years Charlie sang to the horses and cattle.

In between he drew and painted the things he saw but made no attempt to sell what he painted. His drawing was getting better all the time but he didn't know how to compose a picture and consequently put in too much detail. And he had nobody to criticize his work or to talk to about it or make suggestions.

Charlie was no longer sturdy and chunky: he had grown tall and thin—but still kept his square shoulders and short neck—and life in the saddle had made him, as it did most of them, markedly bowlegged. A photograph taken when he was about twenty-two shows a really ferocious looking young fellow with a big, hard mouth, a prominent chin, wide, high cheekbones and fierce eyes, staring out of the picture. For a short time he cultivated a mustache, but had to cut it off— it was so white, he said, that it made him snow-blind.

Besides his regular painting Charlie did considerable decorating—sketches, usually humorous, presented to saloon keepers, and gifts to various girls in the cribs and "houses." (Out west they didn't crudely call it a whorehouse, just "the house," it being, except for ranch houses and saloons, almost the only house the cowpuncher ever entered.)

Charlie's gifts to the girls were little pictures, brightly colored, even pictures of posies, red roses in full bloom and ferns and stuff, painted on big wooden sugar scoops and other inappropriate articles, all meant to hang up on the wall. They were hung up with ribbons and plush and brass-headed tacks—they were strong on red plush. The ladies treasured them, as is proved by the fact that twenty years later, when I was living with Charlie, suddenly, without warning, there would appear a wooden shovel, platter, scoop, butter barrel or what not, each with its faded little picture, and each accompanied by a middle-aged intensely respectable married woman—they *all* married in the end— who wanted Charlie to touch it up, "You know, brighten it up a little!"

These apparitions filled Mrs. Russell with fury. But she had to be tactful and hurt no feelings and make no enemies, and most of all she had, somehow, to circumvent their insistence that Charlie sign it. They all wanted his name and the buffalo skull. It wouldn't do, Mrs. R. declared, to have some wooden shovel, with a drunken rapture of posies painted on it, turn up at an exhibition.

(There's an untapped field for collectors—I wonder nobody's thought of it.)

Two Great Falls saloons, the Mint run by Sid Willis and the Silver Dollar run by Bill Rance—the latter being the first place I ever saw with the floor inlaid with silver dollars, and it had a clock that ran backwards to read in the mirror up behind the bar—had quite a collection of Charlie's work. Especially a quadruptych (that doesn't sound right—anyhow it was a triptych with *four* pictures) that presented "Just a little sunshine"—a cow puncher riding the range and singing in the sun: "Just a little rain"—the same puncher in a slicker, he and his horse half drowned: "Just a little happiness"—he is in town, sitting, shouting, on the edge of the bed with the girl pulling his boots off: "Just a little pain"— he is back on the range, his horse, in the middle distance, is watching him with surprise, beside him on the ground lie a blue medicine bottle and a syringe he has just dropped, and he is holding on to himself with both hands and jumping up into the air with agony.

This sort of thing too had to be kept out of exhibitions. It isn't always easy being an artist's wife.

But exhibitions came later. For eleven years, 1882-92, Charlie rode the range and got along without a wife to edit him.

I am unable to give lush details of Charlie's love life, for he seldom mentioned it and never in detail. Although I gather from other old-timers that it was not entirely a celibate phase of his development, there is nothing to show for it now except a few of the aforesaid wooden hang-ups.

Those were the big days of the cattle business in Montana, and indeed in the whole West, and Charlie saw the northern part of it every way from the ace. Saw and remembered it in minutest detail, and later on he put it down in pictures. That's why his stuff, like Remington's— but Remington specialized on the army—has such historical significance.

And I, had I had sense enough to ask questions and make a few notes, might have recorded all of it. Nary a note, hardly even a question; apparently I thought my Uncle Charlie was going to live forever.

⋙ 8 ⋘

Charlie's First Commission

In the fall of 1886 there was good grass and nice open weather till Christmas.

When at last the snow came, it came to stay—there was two feet on the level. This is unusual in Montana where snow seldom lies very long in the open. It doesn't melt—nothing melts at thirty below—it just dries up and powders and the wind blows it away—piles it in huge drifts under every cut-bank.

But this winter, the famous winter of '87, it crusted over and stayed. The stage line had to send out men on snowshoes to cut willows and stick them up in the snow to mark the road. In part of the country these willows were still standing in May.

Because there had been such good grass the horses came through the winter fat—they pawed through the crust and kept on eating. But cloven footed cattle can't paw—they just go back in the brush and hump up, tail to the wind, and starve. Which made it nice for the wolves—they too came through the winter fat.

Charlie was wintering with the bunch at the O H ranch.

Jesse Phillips, the O H owner was there and when at last the stage came through from Helena he got a letter from Louie Kaufman, one of the biggest cattlemen in the whole country. Louie asked how the cattle were doing.

Jesse started to write a letter and tell him how tough it was. They were all sitting around the kerosene lamp on the table and Charlie said, "I'll make a sketch to go with it."

Which he did.

"Hell!" said Jesse, "Louie don't need a letter—that'll be enough!"

It was a picture, not much bigger than a postcard, of a Bar-R cow, one of Kaufman's brand, and Charlie wrote under it, "Waiting for Chinook."

The chinook wind is peculiar to that part of the country. You go to bed with everything frozen hard and the snow creaking so that you can hear a man walk half a mile away. Along in the night a queer sound wakes you; it gets louder and louder; you sit up in bed and hear chinook come moaning over the prairie—it has a different sound from other winds —and in half an hour the snow on the roof is melting and the gutters running. By morning the country will be almost bare. *That's* chinook.

But this winter chinook didn't come and the cattle died by thousands.

Though Charlie didn't foresee it, this little watercolor drawing circulated among stockmen everywhere and made him known over the whole Northwest. Indeed, it made him famous.

Years afterward some enterprising person turned it into a postcard, entitled "The Last of Ten Thousand," and it is still in circulation today, long after Charlie's death. In the prairie country you're bound to find it in any rack of cards.

Next year, 1888, Charlie—now twenty-four—went up across the Line into the Northwest Territory with the Blood (Kainah) Indians, one of the three Ootlashoot or Blackfoot tribes, and lived with them for six months. He was friends with a young buck named Sleeping Thunder, and through him the older men of the tribe got to know Charlie and liked him so well that they wanted him to join them and marry one of their women. They thought his drawings a kind of magic medicine, each drawing a spirit picture, a sort of colored shadow, a shadow that lasted.

Because his tight blue riding britches, foxed (reinforced) in the seat with white buckskin, made him look from behind like the rear view of an antelope, they called him *Ah-wah-cons*, which means Prong-horn or Antelope.

That's how most Indians get their names—some peculiarity in looks or speech or action. And that, as told later on, is how Almost-a-woman got his unusual name.

Some Indians get their names in dreams: they go off alone up in the hills, and fast and smoke with the sun and have dreams and visions. If they dream of an animal, they recognize him at once as their totem and take his name.

While Charlie was living with the Bloods he learned a little Pay-gani, and especially he learned Sign Language, and learned it so well that he could talk to any of the prairie tribes. The sign language is something like deaf-and-dumb talk but not spelt out with letters—it's all gestures, little pictures made with the hands. It is much the most remarkable invention of the American Indians—*all* the plains tribes could savvy each other in sign-talk.

Each group of tribes had its own spoken language: they couldn't talk to their neighbors with their lips—they could with their hands.

Charlie could tell a story, make jokes and describe the country he had just traversed and the animals and people he saw, all in sign language. Being an artist and using his hands so well, he was as graceful about it as an Indian—it's fascinating stuff to watch.

An account of a trip, translated into words, all simple declarative sentences, would go like this:

"Long time ago—new grass (spring of the year)—I rope my horse—I fork him." (Forking the first and second fingers of the the right hand over the left wrist as you bestride a horse, the straightened out fingers of the left hand shaping the horse's head, the thumb his ear. As soon as your hand is astride him, the horse jogs off toward the right, shaking his head, twitching his ear—you can almost hear him snort.) "I ride across prairie—I come to foothills—come to mountains—see lake—see boat—get on boat—go up lake—see big house," (The two hands dovetailed together with fingers sticking out straight to show the projecting logs at the corner of a log cabin.) "See many people—not related (a hotel full of strangers) much money—much food—much gambling. I eat—drink—smoke—dance—have a *good* time. Many drinks. (Motion of drinking out of whiskey glass, then the hand, with fingers wiggling upward like smoke, goes up in front of his nose to above his head: i.e., he drinks and gets smoke in his head—he's drunk.) Sun goes down—money gone—I go back in woods—unroll bed—sleep—wake up—hear a little noise—lie still—listen—hear another little noise—no like—sit up—look this way—look that way—look behind me—big eyes in the dark (a ghost, a dead man) Me scared—my heart was on the ground."

All told, every word of it, in gestures. An Indian could do it so fast, and so easily, that the different moves flowed over into each other, continuous motion, a sort of visual music, as if he was playing an unseen instrument.

An Indian, talking his own language, often accompanies it with sign-talk—a running pictorial comment on what he is saying. His hands illustrate, elaborate and reinforce his words.

For a few days after leaving the trading post the Bloods lived high, then they began to run out of white man's delicacies and Charlie went for six months without sugar or salt.

This impressed me immensely when Charlie told it—I could hardly imagine life without sugar or *any*thing sweet.

"I missed the sugar only a few days," said Charlie, "then I got used to it. But I never got used to doing without salt. It got so bad that I dreamed about it almost every night—dreamed of finding a big lump of it. Once I dreamed of walking through a salt mine, the walls and roof of rock salt. I never saw a salt mine but I knew there were places like that and it was certainly real in my dream."

Salt must have a smell for animals because years later when I was up in the Rockies with Charlie he planted a couple of big lumps of rock salt in the hillside next the cabin and in just a few nights the deer came down and licked it. After that, at night we often saw deer in the clearing between the camp and the lake. Once I got up in the dark and went out to the spring to get a drink and walked right onto a buck and two does. I didn't see them till the buck coughed—exactly like a man—and scared me backwards. Then I saw them bounding away through the timber, jumping—floating, really—over the down trees. Except for that cough, they made almost no noise. And their legs so slim you'd think they'd snap at the first jump, and their hoofs so dainty. But in the love moon, the mating season, the buck's hoofs, as sharp as razors, are as dangerous as his horns. You grab him by both horns and think you're safe, but he'll reach up and disembowel you with his hoof.

While he was with the Indians, Charlie saw a lot of the Red Coats, the famous Northwest Mounted—they really wore red coats then, not the miserable khaki they wear now—who were watching the Bloods and occasionally turning them back when they strayed too far off their range. They wouldn't see a red coat for weeks and then some afternoon a solitary trooper would come riding into camp, with his boots shined up and his buttons just so, and they knew they were being watched. The Indians have lived like that for generations—watched and herded around like range cattle—no wonder they act like animals and are cowed and sullen.

When he became an artist, Charlie painted the Red Coats more than once. At the big rodeo in Calgary the

Prince of Wales, now the Duke of Windsor, bought a red coat picture for his Canadian ranch, and when Charlie went to England it was always the red coat pictures that attracted most attention.

Charlie liked the Indian's way of life and had he gone west a few years earlier he would undoubtedly have become a squaw man, like his Bent uncles—and as the Bloods wished —but he came late, he couldn't help seeing that the Indian's day was done, so in the early spring of 1889 he quit the camp and rode back across the Line to join his own people. He was in rags and wore moccasins—his boots had given out —and Monte and Gray Eagle were barefoot. Up near the Tetons he met Horace Brewster who staked him to boots and grub and money, and he went to the Judith and got back his job as a puncher. That same summer the cattle outfits began to move north of the Missouri, and at summer's end Charlie wintered for the last time with Jake Hoover.

Many years later he met Hoover on the Coast, where he had become a boatman and took tourists fishing.

But wherever he went, whether up across the Line with the Bloods, or back in the foothills with Jake Hoover or riding the range with some outfit, or wintering at a ranch house or in town, Charlie always had along a few squares of watercolor paint and in his pants pocket a black lump of wax and in between everything else he was drawing and modeling.

When not in the saddle he seemed to lead a pretty idle existence, but really, though he wasn't aware of it—and though he never considered it work—he was really working hard at what he was meant to do.

He was also beginning to drink pretty hard. But this, of course, only when they were in town; on the range they wouldn't see a town, or even a house for months on end.

And always there was an intermittent flow of little adventures. Not much to read about, most of them, but exciting while they lasted and often dangerous.

Charlie's First Commission

The time, for instance, just after the last Indian war, when Charlie, who had been in town and was riding alone across country to join his outfit, came at dark through thick brush down to a water-hole. It was still dusk up on the level but down in the coulie it was already night. He knew there was water there but he couldn't see anything and had to let the horse find it. A horse can smell water but you can't—not when it's fit to drink.

Down in the hollow when the wind blew west there was a terrible smell—Charlie supposed it must be a dead cow or wolf or something—but the water seemed all right and the horse drank without hesitation; so Charlie did likewise and made camp, and mostly the wind blew the other way.

At dawn he sat up and saw his horse looking fixedly at something, and Charlie looked too and saw what there was to see—back in the brush, which was shoulder high, a dead Indian. Some one had shot him as he came down to drink. The brush propped him up at an angle, almost standing, but his head had fallen back and his eyes were open and staring at the sky. It was summer and the wolves hadn't bothered him.

Charlie didn't collect any souvenirs or stop for breakfast but got out of there, quick. Other Indians might happen along, and he didn't feel easy till he had put miles between him and the dead man.

Charlie didn't always get off unmarked. Once when they were either branding or cutting—I forget which— a steer, roped by the forefoot by another puncher, fell against Charlie and drove the sharp tip of its horn right through his boot and instep and into the ground, and wedged the toe bones apart so wide and so painfully, that for years afterward he walked lame. Half a generation later, when I knew him and it had long since stopped hurting, he still out of habit, favored that foot a little.

71

There were endless incidents like that: every once in a while somebody got hurt, and occasionally somebody got killed.

Speaking of cutting, you may think that a steer, castrated in early adolescence, could not have much love life. But in large herds there will often be a young bull or two who is somehow overlooked and escapes the knife, and when he matures and starts sniffing around for a lady, if he can't find a cow he will finally pick on a steer—if you can't get boots you must wear shoes.

The steer though emasculated, still has the instincts of a gentleman—he objects, plenty. He refuses to be seduced, so the only thing left is rape. And if you go out on the range and try to rape a longhorn, you'll find it a man-size job, even a bull-size. The victim puts up an astonishing row and the other steers, excited by the noise and the smell of vital juice, go crazy with frustrated desire and begin bawling and squealing. Presently one of them, quite out of his head, tries to climb the bull—who is fully occupied with his victim, a second steer climbs the first; a third the second and so on, and in no time at all you have the whole herd strung out, pick-a-back, in single file; and the bull, up in front, with all that weight on his hindquarters and his belly sagged down almost to the ground, is in a state of mind quite beyond description. You would be too if you tried to do business with a whole football team hanging on behind and yelling and foaming at the mouth.

The whole herd is screaming to heaven, horns are clicking like mad as others rush up to get in on the orgasm, and sooner or later somebody gets gored.

That adds a new smell, and the instant they sniff blood the cattle go crazy in earnest. They gore and trample any steer who gets a drop of blood on him: of course, those who do the goring get bloodied up too and are gored in turn, and what began as rape ends in general massacre.

You can imagine how the range boss and his riders respond to this—if they don't break it up right at the start they are liable to lose a large part of the herd.

The same thing, at least the massacre part, can be started in the dark by a sleepy or careless night wrangler.

In every herd there are a few one-eyed steers—it's easy to get an eye poked out if you go around with a crowd of longhorns—and these one-eyed gentry, not trusting their brethren overmuch, always want to sleep on the edge of the herd where they can keep their one good eye on the others.

They are a nuisance and a trap for the night herder. In the dark his horse accidentally steps on the steer's tail. That hurts, plenty. Mr. Steer says so, out loud, and scrambles up on his feet and in so doing tears the whiskbroom-end— still under the horse's hoof—right off his own tail. That hurts too, and the steer lunges off through the herd, bawling and whipping his flanks with the bleeding stump and spraying the drops all around him.

The cattle nearest him smell the blood and lumber up and take after him, also bawling. In less than a minute the whole herd is up and milling around in the dark, others get stepped on and the massacre begins.

And if you think it's easy to stop a stampede at night— with the chuck wagon and the sleeping riders a mile or two away—you try it!

There are, of course, plenty of other things—lightning for instance—which will start a stampede at night.

People kept open house in the cattle country—the few who had houses—there was social life of a kind, and women were still so rare that a house with a girl in it, even the homeliest kind of girl, never lacked plenty of callers. A lady school teacher, forty years old and with spectacles, would draw men—big husky, *young* men—around her from that whole corner of the state. They would sit around for days, gaping at her and laughing foolishly, and eat up everything in the place.

The Edgars, St. Louis neighbors of the Russell family, had a big ranch in Montana, and Charlie went there as often as he could because of a visiting daughter, Lolly Edgar, whom he thought the prettiest girl he had ever seen. He had lots of competition. The house, a wide, one-story log building with a pole corral in back and a hitching rack fifty foot long in front, had always a bunch of saddle horses before it, standing humped with their tails to the wind.

Riding up to the ranch, Charlie would recognize some of the horses and know who was ahead of him. A strange horse with a fancy rig and silver conchos on the tapaderos (the big leather stirrup-flaps) would make him bristle up like a dog's hair—some pretty boy from an outside outfit was in.

Charlie wanted to marry Lolly, and she, like Barkis was willin': but old man Edgar horned in and sent her home to St. Louis. He wasn't going to let any daughter of his marry a no-good cow puncher like Charlie Russell. Charlie never forgot her.

Years later, when Charlie married, his wife, herself a very pretty girl, was always just a bit jealous of Lolly Edgar. Charlie had once made the unfortunate remark that he didn't like girls with meaty noses. Mrs. Russell, with a trim old-fashioned figure and curves and so forth, applied this to herself—which Charlie hadn't meant at all—and ever after pictured Lolly as a Grecian goddess, a willowy Artemis with a non-meaty nose.

One wonders what sort of mental picture she had of Lolly, whom she had never seen.

When *I* saw Lolly—she being then middle aged, married and with a whole flock of kids—she was still very fine looking.

Another time—this was before Lolly left and years before Charlie married—there were St. Louis guests at the Edgar ranch, a Captain George Kerr, his stepdaughter, and his niece, the niece being related to Charlie by marriage, her elder sister having married Charlie's elder brother Bent, the gadget engineer. Both daughter and niece were pretty and there was a regular concourse at the ranch, people coming in from miles around just to look at the girls.

Captain George (Confederate), an impressive old party with money, high flown Southern manners, and—when he was crossed—such a majestic and even awful bearing that the family in private called him the Royal Gorge, had gathered that Charlie Russell was the black sheep of his tribe, a ne'er-do-well, a waster, a rover and, in short, a drunken bum. He wasn't at all sure he wanted the girls to meet him.

But when they met—after all the Captain had been through four years of Civil War and knew a man when he saw him—he was so impressed that he ordered an oil painting and asked what it would cost. After some complicated mathematics Charlie named a very modest figure; about enough to pay for stretching the canvas, the paint and three new brushes, and a round of drinks for the house.

"Oh, I'm sure that isn't enough!" said the Captain, and doubled the price.

This was Charlie's first real commission.

The picture, "Counting Coup" (but they pronounce it Koo—it's French Canadian and means a blow) and reproduced later under the caption "When Sioux and Blackfeet Meet," shows how Charlie's friend, Chief Medicine-Whip of the Bloods, got his name by riding in among the Sioux and hitting the Sioux medicine-man with his quirt.

Captain Kerr was my mother's uncle and when he moved to the Coast he gave the picture to her and it hung for years in our diningroom in St. Louis. It has good drawing and action but is so different in color from his later style that you would hardly think it Charlie's work.

(Speaking of style: just last year I saw in a show window on Park Avenue, two small oils which bore Charlie's name and buffalo skull but were manifest forgeries. One, a fight with rustlers, was copied from a larger original but the forger had put a blue waterhole in the foreground. The other, a mountain lion, was striking and mysterious looking, but—Charlie didn't paint it. The storekeeper, of course, didn't know they were fakes. Joe de Yong writes me that he has seen quite a number of faked Russells on the coast.)

You can imagine what sort of notions were put into Charlie's head by getting all that money for doing what he would have done for nothing.

It was then that he began to think seriously of setting up as an artist.

According to common report the left wing of Price's army (Confederate) migrated to Montana after the Civil War, and among them so many from the Mule State that to admit you came from Missouri made people grin. The saying ran, and still runs today, "Not all Missourians are horse thieves, but all horse thieves are Missourians."

Horse stealing was the most serious crime in the cattle country and was always punished by hanging. Which is easy to understand as a man set afoot on the prairie can starve or die of thirst, and also it isn't safe to let range cattle see you out of the saddle. Used from birth to men on horseback, they don't know what you are and may attack you. And, of course, when there was trouble with Indians or outlaws, a man caught afoot was helpless.

Among the Missourians, and inspired by Charlie's adventures, his brothers and cousins also went west: Bent to California as a mining engineer, and Ed, the best looking and tallest of the family, first to Montana with Charlie, where he punched cows on the spring and fall roundups, and then to Nevada prospecting. But Ed was better educated than Charlie; he saw that prospecting was mere luck, mostly hard luck, so he quit adventuring and went back to St. Louis to sell fire brick and special shapes for the Parker Russell Company. Ed was engaged to marry the younger sister of Bent's wife, when he died, still young, of pneumonia. Wolfert, the youngest of the five brothers, was already dead, and Guy died three years later. Thus there remained only Bent and Charlie.

Charlie had a prosperous cousin, Chiles Carr, a big, tall, slim, fine-looking fellow (his grandfather, old Judge Carr, built the first brick house in St. Louis and gave Carr Park to the city) and Chiles had a ranch in Montana where he kept open house and lived and drank in a sort of feudal splendor, and had all kinds of friends until his money gave out.

At that time Charlie was working for the Lazy K outfit and when Chiles went broke, Charlie got him a job as a rider.

Right from the jump the job went wrong. The foreman was a tough-talking proposition and when they went out in the pole corral to get their horses—the company provided each rider with a string of horses—Chiles, who could ride but was used to having a ranch-hand saddle up for him, missed his throw. The horses, of course, were skittish, dodging and plunging and bunching up the way they always do, and Chiles' loop, instead of settling neatly over the horse's head and around his neck, fell on his back and slid off over his hindquarters. The horse snorted derisively and got away.

The foreman snorted too: "Don't look like much of a rider to me! Or do you always catch 'em by the tail?"

Instead of turning it off with a joke or an alibi or just ignoring it and trying again, Chiles put on a spoiled baby act and quit right there.

Charlie felt bad about it and would have fixed it up, but fate and a too convenient saloon gave Chiles no second chance.

By night he was roaring drunk, and having spent his last dollar he climbed into saddle—he still owned a horse—and struck out, howling, across the prairie, spurring at every jump.

That's the last the bunch at the saloon saw of him, and when he was gone from sight they could still hear his voice, shouting his defi to heaven.

Heaven called his bluff. In the dark he ran his horse over a cut-bank. They fell thirty feet, turning over in the air, the horse fell on top of Chiles, and the steel horn of the saddle crushed his life out.

Next morning Charlie and the bunch found them, the horse standing disconsolate with drooping head, trailing reins and a broken leg, and Chiles dead under the cut-bank.

Warning Against Marriage

In the spring of 1889 Charlie went back to the Judith, to his old job of wrangling. Horace Brewster was the captain, the same man who hired him on Ross Fork in '82. A long generation later, Horace Brewster would ride horseback after Charlie's coffin. All those years Charlie had been watching and drawing the kinds of people he met, and the animals and the country. He had no intention of making a record, he didn't know there was any historical importance to what he was doing; he supposed, as did everyone else, that the cattle business would go on forever. Actually the big days of the cattlemen were over inside of twelve years.

But now the West was changing fast. Stage lines, freighters, steamboats and the constantly lengthening railroads were pouring white men into Montana.

Charlie saw the change and didn't like it. By '89 the Judith Country was pretty well settled and sheep had begun to take the range and drive out the cattle. Sheep can graze after cattle, but cattle and horses can't graze after sheep. The woolies, nibbling everything right down to the roots, leave the country as bare as a table. Charlie saw that the Judith was spoiled and followed the cattle north to the Milk River country.

But the sheep and the nesters (small farmers) were hot on his heels. It was evident that in only a few years the cattle and cattlemen would follow the Indians—out.

In the fall of '91—he was now twenty-seven—Charlie got a letter from Pretty Charlie Green, a professional gambler, offering him room and grub and seventy-five dollars a month if he would come to the new town at Great Falls on the Upper Missouri. And all he had to do was paint pictures and model things in wax.

It sounded good—the puncher's problem was always how and where he would live through the winter—so Charlie packed Monte and saddled up his gray and took the trail.

It was a very dry fall and as hot, almost, as midsummer. At noon on the second day Charlie crossed a creek—the last water for at least another six hours—but it had stopped running, nothing left but puddles, and smelled so bad that the horses just sniffed it and cooled their feet but wouldn't drink.

The creek bed was down in a deep coulie with the shore stepped back in terraces. Scrambling up a steep cut-bank on the other side they came onto a flat, waist-deep in dry grass. The grass had been tramped down in a wide circle—just the way dogs do—and lying there, panting with the heat and lolling out their tongues, were a dozen wolves.

Charlie had often killed wolves when he was with Jake Hoover—every once in a while they had caught one in their traps—and he and other punchers had roped and dragged wolves out in the open; except afoot and in winter, he wasn't afraid of them. But horses are—in the wild state the wolf is the horse's only dangerous enemy—and coming on them suddenly that way without warning, Charlie wasn't at all sure what his two horses would do. Most likely they would stop short and fall backwards down the cut-bank. And a horse falling over backwards is almost sure death for the rider—before you can swing out of saddle the horn will get you. So Charlie had reason to be scared.

However, Monte and the gray were both range horses. They pricked their ears and snorted and shook their heads but went on with a rush right through the wolves and scrambled up the next bank onto the open.

"What did the wolves do?" I asked when Charlie told about it.

"Just showed their teeth and grinned, and one, a big dog wolf, sat up and snarled; but they didn't try to follow us. They might in winter, but probably they weren't hungry. Just the same I was damn glad to get up onto the open, and as soon as we hit the level both horses broke into a run."

Getting no drink at the creek and short of food, Charlie traveled light and fast, trying to make a water hole he knew about. It was farther than he thought, he got there after dark and noticed that the horses were choosey about drinking, but they *did* drink and Charlie was so dry that he got down on all fours and began to lap it up.

The water didn't smell very good—but it doesn't at that time of year—and he didn't think much about it till he got two or three little soft things on his tongue. He pulled his dusty neckerchief up across his lips—to use as a strainer—and sucked the water through it. At dawn he found a dead cow at the far end of the pond and the water floating-full of maggots—that's what he got in his mouth.

That cow was rather symbolical—one more season and Charlie's life as a puncher would be over. But he still didn't foresee it. He knew changes impended but he didn't know what. Or how soon.

When he had first come to Montana, Charlie had camped one night on the site of Great Falls, and, had he been a prophet, could have taken up land, and—assuming he lived long enough and didn't die of starvation paying taxes—eventually have become a millionaire. For now when at last he came down to the river, Great Falls had become a town. And it would grow: in just a few years it would be trying to take the state capitol away from Helena.

Lewis and Clark on their great trek overland from St. Louis to the Pacific, had also camped near by and named the upper falls—there are three—Black Eagle because of an eagle which circled overhead and lit in a cottonwood on an island out in the river.

The Missouri, you know, is as clear as crystal above its junction with the Yellowstone; it doesn't look at all like the coffee-colored Big Muddy at St. Louis.

The men who founded Great Falls—chief among them Senator Paris Gibson—had enough originality to keep the new town from having a Broadway. It's laid out checkerboard fashion with wide avenues running east and west and cross streets north and south. Except Central Avenue, which divides the town, all the streets and avenues are numbered.

Charlie rode down Central Avenue and turned in at the first information bureau and bought the barkeeper a drink and asked if he knew Pretty Charlie Green.

"The gambellero?" said the barkeep. "Sure I know him. He hangs out at the Brunswick."

Charlie located him and was taken to yet a third bar and introduced to the proprietor, his prospective employer. Who pulled a contract as long as a stake rope and proposed that they sign it right then. The contract ran for one year: Mr. X was to house, feed and pay Charlie, and Charlie was to work from six A.M. to six P.M. and everything he modelled or painted belonged to Mr. X.

Charlie was no business man and never would be but he was not a damn fool. He pointed out that painting was different from sawing wood, so the contract fell through and Charlie was left flat. It was an anxious moment; he had quit his job just at the wrong time of year to get another and he didn't know what to do. However, he rustled around and found a couple of cowpunchers, a round-up cook, and an out-of-work prizefighter, and between them they scraped together enough to hire a shack on the South Side. As Charlie said afterwards, sometimes the feed was pretty short, but they wintered. Anyhow it was better than riding the grub-line.

Riding the grub-line, cowpunchers called it, when you wintered, free, at ranch houses. Custom required that you stay only three nights at each house and then move on to the next.

Charlie and the prizefighter got crosswise over a girl, and the fighter began telling people what he was going to do about it. Charlie knew better than to exchange fisticuffs with a professional. He got out his equalizer, a big, showy, nickelplated six-shooter with a carved grip, and went where the pug was. He didn't make any warlike talk or offer to use the gun, but the pug saw it and there was no fight.

This was the only time Charlie ever had to pull a gun on a man.

You have heard, of course, the old rhyme about the equalizer which was engraved on many revolvers:

"You need not fear a man
Who walks beneath the skies,
Though you be weak,
And he be strong,
I will equalize."

This same lean winter Charlie met a tenderfoot, new come to the Falls, a man half a generation older than himself, Albert Trigg, who was to become his best friend. Years later, when I lived in Montana, Charlie was at Trigg's house, or Trigg at Charlie's, four or five nights every week.

Next spring Charlie went back to the Milk River country and his last job as night-wrangler for the Bear Paw Pool, but at the summer's end he returned to Great Falls and started painting pictures for a living: and though he had a hard time for many years—just barely made enough to keep alive—he never again rode the range.

CHARLIE RUSSELL, *Cowboy Artist*

This was 1892 and Charlie was twenty-eight.

Charlie never read any of our modern handbooks on how to improve your approach, make friends and get rich, but like high-proof goods he mellowed with age and by the time he reached thirty, people had entirely forgotten "that ornery Buckskin Kid" stuff and thought of Charlie Russell as not only a good mixer but a wonderful story teller—he could keep the whole house laughing all evening. He could be coarse in coarse company, but it wasn't a cruel kind of humor; although a master of ironical statement, he was seldom sarcastic or cynical. But being a good mixer has grave disadvantages, especially in a frontier society where so much of the mixing is done in saloons.

In September 1895 Charlie got a real order—for *three* pictures. He was living in Great Falls and he knew that if he stayed there it would take months to get the pictures done. He also knew he was drinking too much. How could he help it when every old-timer who came into town immediately looked up Charlie Russell—and every new-timer wanted to be introduced? And every introduction meant the stranger buying Charlie a drink, Charlie buying back, anybody else who happened in buying for both of them, and they reciprocating, and so on and so on. A good time was had by all but under this system you don't get much painting done.

Old Doc Sweet had told him straight and plain, "Charlie, you better stop it—whiskey and paint don't mix. You're going to get the shakes, and then where'll your drawing be? You can't keep on drawing and drinking!"

Charlie knew he was right: he had already had one attack of the shakes—his hand jumping so that he couldn't draw—and it had scared him badly. And he had long since reached the point where if he didn't get a drink every so often, he missed it. And that's no way to be when you've got an order for *three* paintings.

84

He knew it wasn't going to be easy to stop—he'd seen too many of the older men try—and he knew it would be impossible as long as he stayed in the Falls.

But he had one real advantage—he was still bull-headed. And it is a great advantage, when you've got to stop drinking, to have a mouth and chin and jaw like Charlie's.

So in October he bought a last round of drinks and announced that he was going to Cascade to visit the Robertses, whom he had known ever since he first landed in Helena in 1880.

"Cascade is no place to sell paintings," said sage old Doc Sweet, swaying perilously and getting a fresh grip upon the bar. "What you need is a business manager. Why don't you stop drinking—stop it *now*—and go home to St. Louis and get one of your brothers or somebody who knows something to handle your paintings for you. That's what you need—a manager!"

The Word creates: a thought put into words is half begun—of course it's the easy half.

Charlie, though he didn't know it, was going to get a manager. But he didn't go to St. Louis, instead he set out for Cascade.

The Robertses had living with them a girl from Kentucky named Nancy Mann, but the kids for some kid reason called her Mamie. She wasn't exactly a servant, and of course in those days they didn't call her a maid, not in Montana, but she helped out in the kitchen and with the kids and Mrs. Roberts gave her a home. She had no home of her own. Her mother was dead and her stepfather had taken her little half-sister and gone out to the Coast and left Nancy behind in Montana.

Nancy couldn't remember Kentucky; all she knew was the prairie country and the foothills. She was young, plump, blonde and quite pretty in a round-faced way, and much

85

excited by the coming of so famous a guest as Charlie Russell. Ma Roberts told her to watch out.

Every time Nancy said anything about Mr. Russell, or even looked like she was going to say something, Ma Roberts told her, "You watch out!"

For Charlie, though no rounder—except in saloons—had what he called a fuzzy reputation.

At sundown, just as Nancy and Mrs. Roberts were getting supper on the table, they heard spur rowels jingling on the back steps and Pa Roberts brought his guest into the kitchen.

This is how Nancy described him many years after:*

"Charlie and I were introduced. The picture that is engraved on my memory of him is of a man a little above average height and weight, wearing a soft shirt, a Stetson hat on the back of his blonde head, tight trousers, held up by a 'half-breed sash' that clung just above the hip bones, high-heeled riding boots on very small, arched feet. His face was Indian-like, square jaw and chin, large mouth, tightly closed firm lips, the under protruding slightly beyond the short upper, straight nose, high cheek bones, gray-blue deep-set eyes that seemed to see everything, but with an expression of honesty and understanding. He could not see wrong in anybody. He never believed any one did a bad act intentionally; it was always an accident. His hands were good-sized, perfectly shaped, with long, slender fingers. He loved jewelry and always wore three or four rings. They would not have been Charlie's hands any other way. Everyone noticed his hands, but it was not the rings that attracted, but the artistic, sensitive hands that had great strength and charm. When he talked, he used them a lot to emphasize what he was saying, much as an Indian would do."

---

* Quoted from *Good Medicine*, Garden City Publishing Co., 1929.

Warning Against Marriage

They met in 1895; Nancy was sixteen and Charlie thirty-one; both blonde and both ignorant. But ignorance, especially Nancy's kind of ignorance, is plastic.

They were both warned not to marry. The Cascade doctor, an old-timer and a friend of many years, told Charlie, "Dont marry that Mann girl. She's a nice little girl, and she's pretty, but she's got a bad heart—she'll be dead inside three years. I know! Anything happening, the least little excitement, may kill her at any moment. You've never seen her faint, have you? Well, she does—just keels over, *bam!* flat on the floor. And that's her heart!"

Practically everybody warned Nancy. They pointed out —it didn't need much pointing—that Charlie drank. And he'd never made a decent living. He was just a common puncher, he had no ambition, he'd never be a boss, much less an owner. The only thing he'd ever owned was a saloon—and all Montana knew how *that* ended.

❧ 10 ❧

Charlie Acquires A Manager

It took Charlie months to make up his mind, and when he finally asked Nancy she refused. He took her for a walk at sunset, they went down by the river and crossed the echoing wooden bridge, and on the bridge he proposed, and she said No.

Years afterward he made a little water-color of it—an autumn evening, the sky darkening to night, a cold wind blowing, and they have just left the bridge. Nancy, downcast, is walking in front with her hands in a muff, her coat buttoned up tight and a little black hat on her head. Charlie following close behind with his coat blown open and sash and white shirt showing—unlike most punchers he never wore a vest—his arms extended in a pleading, persuading, arguing gesture, his hat on the back of his head. That's all there is to it; not much of a picture, but it tells the story.

In the end of course she said Yes.

Then it was Charlie's turn to get cold feet, but he was too much of a gentleman to back out. For Charlie, though not much of a gambler, never welched on a bet.

Charlie and Nancy had met in October 1895, and they were married in September '96. It was not an expensive marriage and they went on no honeymoon trip. Between them they had just seventy-five dollars—mostly Charlie's—with which they furnished a one-room shack in Cascade, which is still standing.

Charlie Acquires A Manager

This gives you an idea how practical Charlie was, Cascade being a quite impossible place for an artist to make a living.

With his wife it was not so much a question of being practical as of being entirely inexperienced. She didn't know anything except how to cook.

Nancy was then seventeen, a pretty little blonde girl, plump and squeezable, with an attractive laugh and nice manners—and very little education—with nothing whatever to show that she was as smart as a steel trap and as quick as the lash of a whip. She didn't know it herself—hadn't the least suspicion.

But it all came out afterward when she began living with Charlie. For Charlie—without intending or even knowing it—was a releasing sort of person. You could see it all the time. In his presence people musclebound with timidity and self-centeredness, relaxed and became at ease. Perhaps it was merely because Charlie himself was always so at ease and so natural, or, as they say nowadays, so well-adjusted.

Which, according to modern psychology, is proof positive that Charlie was not a real artist. Say the psychologists, blow high, blow low, come rain, come snow, no artist can ever be well-adjusted. Why? Because if he did get adjusted he would cease producing art. Charlie knew nothing about all this; such notions were entirely out of his ken.

Charlie was so hopelessly foolish, backward and old-fashioned that he thought art a gift, the implication being a gift from Heaven. Of course, he didn't put it that way—he called it luck. He hadn't earned it, he said, he didn't deserve it, he just had it. Which was indeed the common attitude of artists at the time. The more high-flown artists thought themselves inspired, but Charlie just called it luck.

Of course, even fortunate people have their disappointments. Charlie and Nancy wanted to have a baby, but never did. In this world you can't have *all* the luck.

They lived at Cascade a year, but it was much too small a place to support an artist, so they pulled up stakes and moved to Great Falls—itself no metropolis, considerably less than ten thousand population—but a branch of the Great Northern (Jim Hill's railroad) ran through it and brought a steady trickle of prospective settlers, adventurers, tourists, and people with money. Charlie met most of them at the Silver Dollar or the Mint and once in a while somebody bought a picture. But he was too modest. The prices were really pitiful. And there were times in between windfalls when nobody bought a picture; and then, as Charlie said, "The grass wasn't so good."

His best outlet was black-haired Charles Schatzlein who ran an art store—picture frames, paint, glass and so forth —in Butte, Montana, the big, bad, drunken, gambling, labor-trouble town where the copper smelters are. More than once Schatzlein's orders paid the rent and brought in food just as Charlie was about to give up art and go back to the range.

Said Schatzlein, taking dinner at the Russell shack, "Your price is too low. Out of that last bunch you sent me I sold one for enough to pay for all six. Which makes it nice for me—and anybody else who sells your stuff—but *you* ought to get more out of it. You're no salesman—why not let Nancy handle that end?"

Charlie did; he always hated to tell people how much a picture was worth. Nancy took hold of things, the tariff went up a little and behold, business began to improve. In accordance with a mysterious law of economics, the demand increased with the price.

But at first they were very timid about it and debated for days how much they dared ask for each picture. Neither knew a thing about Art with a capital A; neither had ever met a professional artist. They just went at it blind.

Charlie Acquires A Manager

"Dog-ignorant," Charlie said, "that's what we were."

But they got along: very gradually the prices—and the market—improved and they began to live a little better.

The St. Louis Russells feared Charlie had married a squaw, a halfbreed or something, and when at last he brought her home on a visit they were a bit uneasy; they didn't know what to expect. The ladies wondered if they would have to put up a tent in the backyard, or maybe a cage. They were exaggerating, of course, but we kids took such talk at face value, sitting open-mouthed around the table, listening to our elders and anticipating marvels.

This was Charlie's first exhibition: he exhibited his wife. A successful exhibition. The family approved her at sight though they were shocked by her English, which was worse than Charlie's, and amused by her clothes and by her ignorance of everything they thought important—a comfortable amusement spiced with superiority and condescension. But they found her very adaptable. Much more so than Charlie. A girl that age is like water; pour her into any pitcher, no matter how convoluted, and she takes the pitcher's shape with effortless ease.

Nancy continually shocked her sisters-in-law. She had never been in a city before and her very first day downtown, her first ride on an elevator, she grabbed herself with both hands and exclaimed, "Oo! my stummick!—it felt like it fell out!" (In those days stomach was an obscene word, not used in mixed company.) "But," her sister-in-law remarked that evening, "she looked so pretty that every man in the cage thought I must have said it."

Thus Nancy, floating through St. Louis like a fish through new waters, surprised at what she saw but soon at ease, sure of herself and Charlie. Which she pronounced "Cholly."

Charlie too shocked the family more than once. His sister Sue—now Mrs. Portis, her husband the son of Judge Portis, an old-fashioned southerner from Alabama—took them to some light opera, *Patience* perhaps, and Nancy sat through it like a little lady but Charlie escaped at the first intermission and didn't come back. There was some sort of carnival on a vacant lot at the corner and Charlie took in the freaks and watched Bosco the Wonder eat snakes alive, and was waiting at the theater door when the family came out. Sue, the highbrow of the tribe and herself a bit of an artist, forgave Charlie everything except the snake eater.

This was not mere crudeness on Charlie's part; he really didn't like opera. For, just as some people are color-blind, Charlie was tone-deaf. To him music was just noise.

Except for a few range-songs ("My name it is Joe Bowers/I got a brother Ike," and "Sam Bass was born in Injiana/It was his native home") the only song I ever heard him sing was:

"I've never forgiven that blaggard Pat Shay
Since the time that he ruined me life,
I trayted him daycent, I thought him me friend
Till he up and he stole way me wife."

and the refrain, making his voice growl:

"Now if ever I lay eyes upon the bandy-legged robber
I'll avenge me Irish honor if I hang that very day,
I'll shoot him, I'll cut him, I'll club him, I'll garrote him;
I'll never slape a wink until I murder Paddy Shay."

In those days cigarets were considered disgraceful, a sure sign of vice and crime. They didn't become respectable until the First World War. Even after all these years I still remember the strange, new, almost magical smell of Uncle Charlie's Bull Durham tobacco. He was the first person I ever saw roll a cigaret.

But he was strange in every way. He wore high-heeled boots, a big hat, no vest—a startling innovation. All the men

I knew wore vests even in the St. Louis summer. Instead of suspenders he held up his pants with a halfbreed sash, a Hudson Bay sash, nine feet long. And he didn't tie or buckle it, just tucked it like the latigo on a cinch—give it a jerk in the right direction and it came loose. Also he carried no handkerchief. In the morning he snuffed handfuls of cold water up his nose, and snorted it out again—as a horse does at a river on a dusty day—and that sufficed. I tried it faithfully for weeks but it just wouldn't work; I had to carry a hanky.

In his pants pocket Charlie always had a lump of bees-wax, mottled black from handling, and while he was talking he would take it out and work it soft and model a pig or a buffalo or what not, and look at it in an inquiring way and then mash it out with his thumb and make something else.

He took me to see Ben Hur and the famous chariot race and afterward he modelled me a quadrigga, a four-horse chariot, mounted on a block of wood and painted and gilded. It had lots of action but the horses were right off the range and ran with their heads up and their tails flagged in a manner most unclassical.

I too aspired to be an artist, and Charlie, inspecting my work, remarked, "The kid draws entirely by ear—he never looks at what he's drawing."

Which perhaps is why my aspirations never bore fruit. I favored bare-legged tribes, Greeks, Romans, Indians and so forth, and Charlie called my men the Round-Legs. He said I must have got my ideas of masculine architecture from the beef-trust girls in the *Police Gazette*. But this seems unlikely—the only place I ever saw the *Gazette* was at the barber's, and I wasn't, as yet, old enough to draw ladies.

This trip to St. Louis enlightened Nancy in more ways than one and when they went back to Great Falls she was much bolder in fixing picture prices. And the demand still improved with the price.

They actually began to save a little money.

Of course, there were plenty of rebuffs and disappointments, and sometimes a small success led to a large failure. For instance, they were much thrilled when a real New York editor, William Bleasdell Cameron, visiting Montana, ordered several black-and-white illustrations for *Field and Stream*. They had broken into the magazine game! And made what seemed to Charlie a lot of money. But, though people liked the drawings and wrote in about them, and though they resulted in orders from other editors, in the end they gave Charlie a black eye. For when Nancy finally prodded him into holding his first exhibition in St. Louis, the Art Museum refused to buy any of Charlie's paintings, because, as they explained, he was only an illustrator, not a real artist. Besides he had never studied in Europe nor lived in New York. Neither would they let him exhibit under their auspices.

This was a real shock to Charlie who had supposed that just as a matter of course St. Louis, his own home town, would be glad to show his work.

He didn't know St. Louis.

Charlie was almost sick about it—he wondered if he really was an artist or just a sort of faker.

But Nancy was of sterner stuff. It made her fighting mad.

The St. Louis Museum still has none of Charlie's work and is proud of it—a prophet in his own country and so forth. They have several of Remington's paintings, his contemporary. But Remington came from New York.

As another artist remarked in the *St. Louis Post Dispatch*, in St. Louis art is on the bum.

However, there seemed to be quite a lot of people who didn't care what the Art Museum thought. They crowded the exhibition at Strauss' gallery and bought a number of paintings and the papers gave it a big write-up.

This encouraged Nancy to try exhibitions in Denver and Chicago and finally—1903—in New York. All succeeded; all got good notices; all paid expenses, and some paid a profit.

Before he married, while he was still punching cows, Charlie had been to Chicago several times, riding the cattle-cars armed with a pole to prod the steers up on their feet when they lay down, this to keep the others from trampling them. So he felt sort of acquainted with Chicago. But he didn't like New York: it was too crowded and too lonely. Till they began to get acquainted they were terribly lonely. And at first the hotel cowed him.

Nancy stood it better than Charlie. She was fifteen years younger and a hundred times more adaptable; and she was the nervous, excitable, energetic kind. Right from the start she went out determined to meet people, important people, the kind of people who could help Charlie along. It was quite an undertaking for a girl so ignorant and so unsophisticated. And at first it was very exhausting, even for her energy.

But she kept on. She might—she often did—have stage fright; she might—she often did—have a fainting spell after the crisis was over, but while the battle went on, she was in there slugging. Her youth and appearance helped: it was a very unobservant art editor, critic, or dealer, who didn't notice how young and pretty she was. And how unsophisticated. Several tried to date her.

Nancy's ignorance played right into their hands. Not knowing the gentlemanly New Yorker and how his brain works and how easy it is for a girl, any girl, to convince him forever—just give him a big-eyed look and say, "Well you sure surprise me!"—convince him forever that he's *the* original wolf, she got more than once into embarrassing and even painful situations, but always extricated herself with the forthright directness which a girl can show if she wants to.

Excited by what they thought the narrowness of her escape the wolves naturally tried again, but upon meeting Charlie they always remembered that great American adage, Safety First, and looked elsewhere for their dates. So Nancy found New York distinctly exciting.

Then, too, she was interested in shops and clothes—Charlie wasn't; she learned how to use the elevated—Charlie didn't. She went around crashing gates and looking up people —Charlie either tagged along reluctantly or stayed in the hotel.

One rainy afternoon when his active half was out battling for recognition, Charlie was reduced to such straits that he opened the Gideon Bible and read quite a little of the early part, the wars and adventures of the Chosen People, and was surprised to find it so interesting. He concluded that the Hebrews were a ferocious bunch—"Hew Agag in pieces before the Lord"—and he sympathized with Hagar, and Ishmael, and Esau, but took a dislike to Jacob, the pious sharpshooter who went around getting the best of his relatives.

Who knows, Charlie might have got religion, but just then success came tapping at the door—or, rather, Nancy dragged success in, hog-tied and branded, and as far as I know Charlie never opened the Bible again.

At first it was a very modest success. No sudden storybook triumph. But they did sell six large paintings, oil, and a number of water colors for twice what they had ever got before. And they did begin to get recognition from the critics, they did meet art dealers and art buyers with money.

People are queer: The thing that pleased Charlie most and amused him and flattered him happened while they were sitting in the lobby of the swankiest hotel they had yet been in, waiting for some art biggie—I forget who—to come downstairs. Nancy noticed that the bellhops over on their bench were looking at Charlie and having a big argument about something. Presently the littlest came over and said, "Mister, would you settle a bet for us?"

"Sure," said Charlie, "what is it?"

"One of the boys says you're Frank Gotch, and the other says you ain't."

Gotch was then the champion wrestler. He didn't really look at all like Charlie, but all the bell hops noticed Charlie's build.

And now for the first time, thanks as always to Nancy, Charlie began to meet professional artists and go to their studios and offices—some had studios, some had offices—and watch them at work, and show them his, and get their comments and criticisms.

At first they were mostly illustrators, newspaper and magazine men and advertising artists: Marchand, for instance, did westerns; Gus Mager, comics; Joe Schuerle and the youthful Philip Goodwin, did circus posters; the two Kinneys; Glachens, Schreyvogel, Schoonover; Bill Krieghoff, who wanted to be—and later became—a portrait painter, but was then working for Outcault Comics (the Yellow Kid, Buster Brown and so forth); and especially Will Crawford, the pen-and-ink man. Krieghoff told how he saw some newspaper artist inking in while the copy boy tapped the edge of the drawing board with a ruler—he was trying to get a shaky Will Crawford technique.

Charlie was surprised, taken aback, and occasionally offended by the extreme directness and frankness with which some of the more coarse-minded and heavy-handed of these people criticized his stuff and pointed out just what they didn't like. But he was no Chiles Carr; he could take adverse comment with a wooden face and say, "I guess you're right."

Much of this adverse comment was good—just what he needed—and he knew it, and even when it made him sore, he used it.

Occasionally Charlie turned the tables and criticized *their* work.

The western artist, Albert T. Reid—born in Concordia during the Indian wars when Colorado was still part of Kansas—tells how he met Charlie in New York about 1906. At that time there was a three-story brick studio building on the northeast corner of 40th and Broadway, and Marchand's studio was on the third floor. Reid and Arthur Jamieson, the Hearst artist, went to visit Marchand.

Climbing the steps, they saw a bridle and headstall on the newelpost, a stock-saddle on the bannister and in the saddle a model—but he didn't look like a professional model —with chaps (chaparayos), boots, spurs, and halfbreed sash. It was Charlie posing for Marchand.

Marchand, himself Kansas-born, introduced them, "Charlie, here's a couple of hombres from the home-range," and they went into the studio to look at the picture Marchand was painting. Charlie said, "Marsh, you've got his neck too short—a horse is the same length from the poll to the withers as from the withers to the croup."

"And that," says Reid, "is the very thing I had forgotten. When I was little my mother taught me to draw a horse inside a square, and I remembered all the dimensions except the neck in proportion to the back."

Years later the columnist, Walt Mason, another Kansan, wrote "The West They Knew":

The romance and glamor and men of the West is an epoch of thrills and wonder and awe. It calls for pictures with color and zest, by a fellow who's seen it and one who can draw; who graphically tells of each spirited deed—like paintings by Remington, Russell and Reid.

The old Leather-neck who skippered the stage over prairie and mountain—Saint Joe to the sea; land barren of all except mesquit and sage which screened the wild savage and coyote—for me, my eyes yearn for something on which they can feed—a drawing by Remington, Russell or Reid.

There are plenty good pictures and picture-chaps too—pictures of everything under the sun, but when it comes to the West that I knew, with its redmen and troopers and man with a gun, its stages and drivers and Indian steed—well, I must have Remington, Russell or Reid.

Along with the artists, Charlie began to meet writers and actors, the St. Louisan Augustus Thomas (*Arizona, In Missouri, The Witching Hour*), Caspar Whitney, editor of *Outing*, Emerson Hough, Alfred Henry Lewis of *Wolfville*, Irvin Cobb, Fred Stone and Francis Wilson and Will Rogers—no, he came later, on Charlie's third or fourth trip to New York—and particularly he met Bill Hart, then playing second parts—the wicked villain who gets killed at the end. Charlie saw him first in *Ben Hur* in the famous chariot race in which Bill played Messala, the Roman villain, and quite eclipsed the hero. When they first met, movies and nation-wide popularity had not yet come Bill's way.

Later Charlie saw Bill as Trampas in *The Virginian* and objected to his fake cowboy song, "In gambling hells delay-ing, Ten thousand cattle stray-ing. Sons-of-guns is what I say, They rustled my pile, my pile away." (In those days sons-of-guns was a very bold word to use on the stage.) Said Charlie, "Why didn't you sing a real range song like *Joe Bowers?*"

"Don't ask me," said Bill, "ask the literary artist who wrote it. I'm just the poor villain who gets shot twice a day."

Both Charlie and Nancy were shocked by what Mister Dooley would have called the hootchie-kootchie morals of the East. Charlie was used to rough stuff but not the New York kind with its characteristic smell, and after he had been taken to a few stags, smokers and night-clubs (but they called them cabarets) he concluded that Sodom and Gomorrah had nothing on the big city.

What happened to Lochinvar in a newspaper poem— he went to Chicago and made some tall talk about how wild he was and got acquainted with a gentleman in a derby hat who admired him greatly and bought him a Mickey Finn— might easily have happened to Charlie. But Lochinvar had no Nancy to ride herd on him and see him safe through all temptations.

Charlie had his temptations. One lady, not a professional, propositioned him. She wrote—perhaps modeling herself on that world-shaking work of art *Three Weeks*—that she wanted to have a son as fine looking as Charlie.

I don't know what Charlie did about this, if anything, but years later, when I was in Montana, old man Trigg told about it in my presence and compared Charlie to the farm boy in the great city who was tempted but said No, he had to be true to the Jersey cow.

It cost Trigg fifteen minutes of earnest explanation that he was quoting the farm boy, *not* Charlie, and that he hadn't the least intention of comparing Mrs. R. to a cow. It isn't safe to make jokes like that before ladies, not when they're as touchy as Aunt Nancy.

"Now, Mameso," said Charlie, that's what he always called her when he was smoothing her down, "you know Trigg wouldn't think a thing like that!"

I remember I laughed at the wrong time and got myself disliked.

Charlie Acquires A Manager

Nowadays when you can't walk down any New York street without seeing at least one radio cowboy with boots, a big hat and a guitar—a *guitar,* my God! Charlie wouldn't have been found dead at a dog fight with a guitar—western, or pseudo-western, clothes attract no attention. But in Charlie's day, though there were plenty of synthetic southern colonels, there were few, if any, synthetic cowboys. So Charlie attracted lots of attention: his boots—he wore them inside his pants but they showed—his sash, his soft shirt, his hat, his rings, and most of all his face, made people look at him.

Reading this over I see I have omitted the very thing which most impresses all good Americans, namely, that besides the artistic, literary and theatrical crowd, Charlie met a number of really wealthy people and visited their homes. I remember the names of only two of them, the Risleys and the Mackays. Later he met Dr. P. G. Cole who afterwards made a collection of Russells. Their wealth and their culture —such of them as had it—naturally awed Nancy more than it did Charlie. Yet as soon as she got over her first stage fright, Nancy became more at ease with them than Charlie ever did. He wasn't cowed by their wealth and social position— for which he cared nothing—but he saw that what the Bible has to say about serving Mammon is just as true now as the day it was written, and that nineteen hundred years of Christianity have not had the least effect on the gods of gold and what they do to their worshipers.

Meeting these different kinds of people changed the look of many things for Charlie. He saw his own work in different perspective; he saw mistakes he had been making and which he had been entirely unable to see until other artists pointed them out. He began to correct them.

But the biggest change was in Nancy. She had gone East raw and crude. She came back, not finished—far from

101

it—but wonderfully polished up. Her dress, her talk—both grammar and vocabulary—and especially her way of thinking, all showed the change.

⁓§ 11 ß∂

Charlie Gets A Home And A Studio

In 1900 Charlie's mother died. Three of her children, Ed, Guy and Wolfert, were already dead, so what she left went to Sue, Bent and Charlie. Charlie was then thirty-six.

With this nest egg Nancy—now general manager—bought a big double lot way out on Fourth Avenue North in the best part of Great Falls and began to build a real home, a story-and-a-half frame house with the bathroom downstairs, as it often is in Montana, a big sunlit hall, a great big living-room—they had so many callers—storm windows, double doors back and front, and, in the basement, a real hot air furnace.

They still ate in the kitchen, and Charlie painted in what the architect had called the dining-room.

Out in back on the alley, they had a small corral and a stable with a big hay loft above it for Monte, now sway-backed with old age, and Nee-*nah*, a bay cow-pony. Nee-*nah* is an Indian name, not Mexican, and means "Chief." He too lived to great age.

Years later, when I was living with them, George Calvert, one of Charlie's best friends, a carpenter who had become a contractor, called up one afternoon—I must have been working night shift at the smelter because I was in bed—and when I assured him that both Mr. and Mrs. were out, he appeared in a few minutes—got me up again—and insisted on going upstairs to measure the hall door of the spare bedroom. He acted mysteriously, wouldn't say what it was for, and told me to keep my mouth shut. At Christmas he produced a hardwood door with a full-length plate-glass mirror. I believe that was the best present Nancy ever got—she had wanted one for years.

Later still, another contractor, putting in the new granitoid sidewalk on Fourth Avenue, used his surplus material to make a big ace of diamonds slab, and on it, in color and in high relief, a white buffalo skull with black horns. This he inlaid in the sod on the steep slope up to the front yard of Charlie's house.

Later yet, Nancy built a high retaining wall in front of the whole property, and set upright in the wall this diamond shaped coat of arms. It was, I think, the only piece of heraldry in Great Falls, perhaps in Montana, except, of course, the State Seal.

However Columbus Hospital *did* have an heroic statue out in front—chewing-gum colored—which Charlie called Columbus-with-the-lumps-on-his-legs, because the sculptor hadn't been sure about the calf, whether it came in back, front, or on both sides; so he played safe and gave the discoverer balustrade legs with calf all the way around.

As soon as they had finished the house and furnished it, Nancy began talking about some day building a studio on the other lot. "A place of your own!" she said. "A place where you can work without being disturbed, where you can shut yourself in and shut the world out when you get to 'fighting' a picture," (for Charlie sometimes had trouble with his pictures—the only time he was grumpy and dangerous to disturb). "A place where my friends, and every delivery boy and salesman, won't be bouncing in on you at all hours and expecting you to stop everything and entertain them." (For the milk man, the ice man and so forth felt free to barge in at any time with their friends and relatives and exhibit Charlie like something in the zoo.) "And especially a place where you can have your own friends and talk without needing to whisper the interesting parts because you're afraid I'm in the next room listening. A real studio, with a sky light, that's what you need—and it ought to be all one big room."

This talk made Charlie uneasy. He knew how suddenly Mameso made up her mind, and, once she had made it up, with what furious energy she pushed anything through. Said he, "I'd rather have a plain log cabin, like the one I lived in with Jake, but bigger." Then, realizing that this was dangerous talk, he added, "But, of course, you couldn't build a log cabin in town—people wouldn't like it!"

In 1903, just one hundred years after the Louisiana Purchase—which resulted, among other things, in Lewis and Clark camping on the site of Great Falls—Nancy began to build the studio on the lot next to the house. It was a log cabin, an unusually large one, and set well back from the street.

Here, in her own words is her account of it as given in Good Medicine.

"Charlie did not like the mess of building so he took no more than a mild interest in the preparations. Then, one day, a neighbor said, 'What are you doing at your place, Russell, building a corral?'

"That settled it. Charlie just thought the neighbors didn't want the cabin mixed in with the civilized dwellings and felt sure they would get up a petition to prevent our building anything so unsightly as a log house in their midst. But way down in his heart, he wanted that studio. It was the right kind of work-shop for him, but he was worried at what he thought the neighbors would say, so he would have nothing to do with it.

"He made no further comment, nor did he go near it until one evening, Mr. Trigg, one of our dearest friends, came over and said, 'Say, son, let's go see the new studio. That big stone fireplace looks good to me from the outside. Show me what it's like from the inside.'

"Charlie looked at me kind of queer. The supper dishes had to be washed. That was my job just then, so Charlie took Mr. Trigg out to see his new studio that he had not been in. When they came back into the house, the dishes were all put away.

"Charlie was saying, 'That's going to be a good shack for me. The bunch can come visit, talk and smoke, while I paint.'

"From that day to the end of his life he loved that telephone pole building more than any other place on earth and never finished a painting anywhere else. The walls were hung with all kinds of things given him by Indian friends, and his horse jewelry, as he called it, that had been accumulated on the range, was as precious to him as a girl's jewel box to her.

"One of Charlie's great joys was to give suppers cooked over the fire, using a Dutch oven and frying pan, doing all the cooking himself. The invited guests were not to come near until the food was ready. There was usually bachelor bread, boiled beans, fried bacon, or if it was Fall, maybe deer meat, and coffee; the dessert must be dried apples. A flour sack was tucked in his sash for an apron and, as he worked, the great beads of perspiration would gather and roll down his face and neck.

"When it was ready, with a big smile, he would step to the door with the gladdest call the oldtime roundup cook could give—'Come and get it!'

"There was a joyous light in his eyes when anyone said the bread was good, or asked for a second helping of anything. When no more could be eaten, he would say, 'Sure you got enough; lots of grub here.'

"Then the coffee pot would be pushed to one side, frying pan and Dutch oven pulled away from the fire, and Charlie would get the 'makins.' Sitting on his heels among us, he would roll a cigarette with those long, slender fingers, light it, and in the smoke, drift back in his talk to times when there were very few, if any, white women in Montana. It was Nature's country. If that cabin could only tell what those log walls have heard!"

The same year, 1903, St. Louis intended to celebrate the centennial of the Louisiana Purchase by a world's fair, the biggest yet. It was an ambitious project, the buildings were enormous, they had to dig lagoons and lakes and divert the River Des Peres; and a cumulative collection of delays resulted in the fair not being opened till the spring of 1904. When it did open it was impressive. The great Henry Adams was astonished that a backwoods town inhabited by abject hinterlanders, could put on so good a show.

Nancy had meant to have an exhibition at the Fair and when it was postponed she went ahead and held it anyhow, again not at the St. Louis Museum. The show drew crowds and was a success, they sold a number of pictures, both oil and water color, and the St. Louis papers gave Charlie a big write-up with details about his life, his marriage and so forth, and quite a lot about Nancy. Charlie, as always, gave her all the credit for his success.

They were staying then at our house, 4950 Washington, four doors from the big yellow brick Baptist Church, the church with the campanile, on the corner of Kingshighway.

In those days everything from our back gate south to the millionaire Bixby place on Lindell Boulevard, was vacant lots, head-high in summer with weeds. A jungle with rabbits in it and a pack of wild dogs—at least that's what we called them—they had no home. They killed my dog, Mark Hanna —yellow, named for the Republican Boss. I heard the battle, lying in bed, and knew Mark's warcry, but he was always fighting and I didn't realize this the finish.

All which has nothing to do with Charlie except that he was staying with us when he got that letter which put a new look on Nancy.

12

Nancy Discovers Her Father

At this time there was living in Illinois a Mr. J. A. Cooper, a thin, middle-aged, hard-working, worrying, anxious sort of person, who was running a country hotel in a small town across the river from St. Louis. The kind of man, without training, trade, or profession—and with only a country-boy education—who can go almost anywhere and do almost anything and make a living at it, but who worries about it even while he's making money. Mr. Cooper had never run a hotel before and though the owners were satisfied with his management, it worried him. And he had no family with whom to discuss his worries and was entirely alone.

Now Mr. Cooper came from Kentucky.

After business hours when the colored cook, waiters and dish washer had gone home and the hotel was buttoned down for the night, he read the *Post Dispatch* and saw the big write-up about Charlie Russell, and was so astonished, so shocked, so utterly dumfounded, that it threw him into a fever of anxiety. After thinking it over—he thought about nothing else for twenty-four hours—he sat down and took pen in hand, a scratchy hotel pen, and wrote Charlie a letter. A very anxious letter.

He invited Mr. and Mrs. Russell to come to the hotel as his guests and talk things over. He noted, he said, that the paper gave Mrs. Russell's maiden name as Nancy Mann, and the date of her birth, and the town she was born in, Mannsville, Kentucky, which was named for her grandfather.

All which added up to this: though he, Cooper, had never known he had any children, Nancy must be his daughter. He gave dates to prove it.

A country boy, he had married very young. He and his wife, also very young, lived together only a few months, then they quarreled and he up and quit her. Just hauled out and went to another part of the state. When at last he calmed down and decided to go home, he wrote to his wife. Getting no answer, he wrote to his own family and his brother wrote back that old Mr. Mann had made his daughter get a divorce. The brother, not living in Mannsville, didn't know there was a baby coming, so Cooper—who never went home again but drifted around the southern part of the country, doing all sorts of things and always regretting the way he quit his wife—lived for more than twenty years without knowing he had a daughter.

The other side of the shield is this: soon after Nancy was born her mother married again, a Mr. Allen, who took her and the baby to Montana. Where in due time she bore another daughter, Ella Allen, Nancy's little half-sister.

The two children were still young when their mother died, and Allen, a restless sort of fellow, left them with friends in Montana and went on to the Coast. Where he married again and had another batch of children. When this second wife died, Allen came back to Montana and got Ella, then ten years old, and took her out to the Coast to keep house for him and take care of her little half-brothers and half-sisters.

Nancy, then nearly grown, was left at Cascade with the Robertses and didn't see Ella again for several years. Nancy, of course, could not remember Kentucky and knew nothing except the Montana prairie and foothills. Kids take their surroundings and their family for granted and it never occurred to her to ask about her own father, whom she supposed long since dead. She didn't even know that her name was Cooper: her mother had always called her Nancy Mann.

Well, the short of it was that she and Charlie went to the hotel and stayed overnight with Mr. Cooper and decided that he undoubtedly was her father.

He didn't look at all like her. She was blonde and plump and he dark and thin, but he had the same driving nervous energy, and though the mess he made of his marriage and a lifetime of loneliness had given him an anxious, timid, apologetic look, this timidity never prevented his branching out and trying new things in business and he nearly always made money. He was not the kind who would ever get rich but he did make money. It was an enormous release to him to find that he had a daughter and was not, as he had always supposed, entirely alone in the world.

Naturally he was a little bit timid with her, and especially with Charlie who, in point of age, was about midway between father and daughter.

St. Louis was as far west as Mr. Cooper had ever been, and their westernisms, the way they thought and talked and acted, made them seem almost like foreigners to a Kentuckian.

Later that week he came to our house and met Charlie's family—which must have been quite an ordeal. The only thing I recall about this meeting is the erratic and jerky gesticulation with which he accompanied his words—sheer nervousness and self-consciousness, of course, but I was too young to understand. I just thought him queer. Years later, when I was grown, he and I boarded for a time at the same place in Montana and I found him quite an interesting person, still tirelessly energetic, still branching out and trying new kinds of work—contracting, for instance, about which he knew nothing—still making money at it, and still worrying.

When they finally got acquainted, he and Charlie—though they had almost nothing in common—got along quite well. Feeling himself too old to address him as father, Charlie called him Coop.

Next year, 1904, the St. Louis World's Fair opened, and Mr. Cooper managed a much larger hotel just outside the wall.

This time Charlie had one painting, "Pirates of the Plains," in the Art Palace on top of Art Hill, but this was chosen by the World's Fair commission, not by the St. Louis Art Gallery. He had also many paintings in the Montana State Building.

13

Charlie In Montana

A number of years after Charlie went west, Charles S. Russell, his father (my grandfather), took me on a summer vacation trip to Montana. Charlie's sister Sue and her husband, Tom Portis, went with us. That must have been in 1904, the year of the St. Louis World's Fair.

We went up to St. Paul and thence via the Great Northern to Havre, said to be the coldest place in Montana. A priest stationed there told Charlie, "If I had a house in Havre and another in Hell, I'd sell the one in Havre." In Montana they pronounce it "Hav-errr"—with three or four R's.

Born and bred in Missouri, this was for me a first view of the prairie, and Dakota, as flat and as green as a pool table, with little toy farm houses and enormous red barns, did not look at all like the country Charlie painted.

We were out of Dakota and into Montana—a more rolling and more barren kind of prairie—when we saw our first coyote running away from the train. We also saw, or had pointed out to us, the tremendous changes made by one generation. The buffalo had disappeared entirely, and so had most other game; the English sparrow had driven out the native birds; the prairie sod, once broken by the plow, would not grow again in a thousand years; the tumbleweed—unknown in Charlie's youth—had come in with the wheat, and so had lesser pests innumerable; along the right of way the dandelion was taking everything—and all this the white man had done in one generation.

113

CHARLIE RUSSELL, *Cowboy Artist*

We did not go to Great Falls but straight up to Charlie's summer camp in what is now Glacier National Park but which was then a forest reserve. We went right in among the Rockies but did not see them. There was forest fire somewhere and a thin haze of smoke hid the mountains—all we saw were the foothills. Which looked big to me, the Ozarks and Lookout Mountain in Tennesee being the only mountains I had ever seen.

This was long before the day of air-conditioned trains. The sleeper was hot, and when, after dark, we got off at Belton I was astonished at the mountain air, how cold it was, and how quick, as if alive. It woke you up wide awake and made you tingle. It also made your teeth chatter. I was used on former vacations to the sudden damp chill of the Great Lakes, but that chill, wet and sea-levelish, was quite different from this dry, high—three thousand feet—and sparkling mountain air. You could really feel it sparkle.

After the pintsch-gas light of the sleeper the platform was dark as a cave. All we could see was a dimly lit station and a hill immensely tall against the sky, its top outlined by stars. Ten times as many stars as you see in the Mississippi Valley, and ten times brighter.

Uncle Charlie and Aunt Nancy were there to meet us and hurried us onto the stage, a big farm wagon with benches running from front to back. I sat at the end next the tailgate and got a death-grip on the side, being warned that the road went almost straight up and I might easily be jolted off. There was no broad government highway then, just a dirt track full of ruts.

The stage was so crowded that one of the natives, unable to get a seat, walked all the way behind us with a swinging lantern, which kept me from seeing anything except his feet and legs to the knee and the ground in the circle of light. The pine woods on either side were as black as the pit.

Charlie In Montana

We crossed the Flathead River and climbed the hill—which, like most hills, proved to be not quite as steep as expected—and after a long ride through the woods (nowadays the bus whirls you there in no time) we reached Apgar at the foot of Lake McDonald. At its up-end were the real mountains and Gunsight Pass but we couldn't see them, we saw just the lake, as smooth as a mirror, stretching off into darkness. Except for three log cabins, all dark, and a log postoffice, there was no sign whatever of civilization.

We lugged our suitcases down the beach—not sand but gravel, which made a great clinking and clanking underfoot—and embarked in a rowboat, and Charlie and I took the oars. Charlie was the world's worst oarsman; it was impossible to keep stroke with him. He rowed with a short choppy jerk and every few minutes he let his oars trail and turned around to see where he was going. He never learned—and you couldn't persuade him to try—to set his course by some tree or other landmark astern; he had to keep turning around to look ahead.

We steered cattycorner across the end of the lake and as the shoreline was just an unbroken front of pine trees jagged against the sky, I wondered how we were going to find the landing.

"There it is!" said Charlie, and I saw a dim triangular white thing which seemed to be hovering in the air ten feet above the water.

"Welcome to Bull's Head Lodge!" said Aunt Nancy, and we steered in to a log float. The white thing was a buffalo skull cut out of planks and set up on a pole to mark the landing. Behind it, a steep hundred yards up the hill, was the cabin, and Nancy lit a big railroad lantern—there were no flashlights then—and we went up. As soon as we stepped off the tinkling pebbles of the beach, the ground was covered, inches deep, with a brown and springy floor of pine needles as slick as glass, and shining like bronze in the lanternlight.

There for the first time in my life I slept in a log cabin roofed with "shakes"—big handmade cedar shingles—so loosely laid that you could look up and see the stars between them; and was much impressed by the beds which were hinged to the wall and folded up out of the way. We all slept in the same room, for at that time Charlie had only one cabin where later he built four.

Right beside the cabin, and black and mysterious looking in the lanternlight, was a spring of ice-water. All along that shore of the lake there are springs of ice-water every few hundred feet as if the hill itself was over a glacier.

I could write chapters about the camp and the country and the people we met, both westerners and tourists, but this book intends to deal with Charlie, so I will merely mention the trade-rats who played up on the roof every night and stole our toothbrushes and left pine cones and strips of bark in exchange—that's why they're called trade-rats—and the chipmunks down near the water, and the pine-squirrels who scolded at us on the trails, and the porcupine who hid under the boat and Charlie got some of his quills by flicking him with a gunnysack. We also saw a skunk, very neat and clean looking and very leisurely and sure of himself—we gave him the trail—and we saw several bunches of deer, and a weasel, long and slim and as quick as a flash, who darted out from under a log, and a mother shrew no bigger than your thumb and her microscopic babies. Of course, there were moose back in the beaver-meadows, and bears and timber wolves and mountain lions, but we never saw them. You can live for years in the woods and never see a lion, but if you go hunting in the snow and backtrack the same way you came, just turn off a few paces to right or left and you'll find his prints where he has followed you, off to the side, without ever crossing your trail. It's sort of eerie to know that he is following you but never see or hear him.

Another thing we didn't see for the first couple of weeks was the Rockies. Though we were right in them and though the sky looked clear and the stars shone every night there was just enough haze of forest fire smoke to hide the mountains. At the week's end Aunt Sue and Uncle Tom went on to the Coast, and that night the wind changed, the smoke went back, and next morning when I came down to the shore there were the mountains right at the head of the lake, real mountains, high above timber line and with snow on their peaks. They took your breath. Far off between them we could see the V-shaped notch of Gunsight Pass, and even, when Charlie pointed it out, the edge of the nearest glacier.

Later we went on several pack trips with horses and guides up to Avalanche Basin and other places, and crossed the glacier, and saw the mountain meadows above timberline and their gorgeous flowers, especially the flaming red of the Indian Paintbrush, and the tall white tassel of the Beargrass, and heard the whistling marmots and other wonders: but all of this would be too long to tell and there was nothing new in it to Charlie.

I remember him at our highest camp squatting on his heels before the fire baking bannock-bread in a pan, and the guide—who should have done the cooking—dropping cigaret ashes in the dough—which Charlie said made no difference.

At the summer's end we went back to St. Louis, but two years later we came west again, and two years later still; and the third time I stayed there. Stayed in the mountains all summer and in the autumn went to Great Falls with Charlie.

This must have been 1908 and Charlie was forty-four. Though not fat, he had thickened up and got middle-aged looking.

In 1908 we left the mountains and the foothills and crossed the prairie and drew near Great Falls, and saw, many miles before we got there, the tall brick stack of the smelter, the Big Stack, the biggest, then, in the world. For though Great Falls had no copper mines, it had unlimited water power. The smelter, the Boston & Montana Copper Company, originally independent, was finally swallowed up by Anaconda, the Big Snake, which ruled—and still rules—Montana.

The town itself surprised me. Though built right out on the prairie at the junction of Sun River and the Missouri, it was so hidden in trees that you couldn't see the houses. And every tree had been planted. At that time Great Falls claimed ten thousand citizens. It had already passed Helena and wanted to be the State capital.

After the three-story brick houses of St. Louis, Charlie's one-and-a-half story frame seemed a mere cottage; and the double doors, front and back, and the vestibules and storm windows, gave an idea what kind of winter you could expect on the prairie.

Charlie rebelled at asking anyone for a job but his wife was less sensitive and introduced me to Ed Holland, head of the Townsite Company, who sent me out to the car barns, and I began washing street cars at two fifty per—big wages then, the steel mills back east paying only two dollars for a twelve-hour day.

They broke me in as a motorman and one anxious afternoon I ran a car to and from the big football game. I had been going to games for years but always as a passenger; now I discovered what an ordeal it is for the motorman.

But what impressed me about Great Falls was the people, especially the old-timers, Charlie's friends; they were so different from the people at home, and—as it seemed to my young ignorance—so crude. Spotting me as a pop-eyed tenderfoot, they discoursed to such effect that I concluded all Westerners were liars, *silly* liars.

Charlie seemed to know everybody in town.

Bill Rance for instance, an incorrigible practical joker who ran the Silver Dollar—a regular art gallery of the lighter side of Charlie's work—and Sid Willis who ran the Mint; Eyebrows Conrad, the town's only millionaire; and Old Bob Ford, the banker. (Conrad, according to Charlie, had seen all sorts of interesting things in early days but remembered only the price of buffalo hides, the price of this, the price of that; whereas his contemporary and rival, Old Bob Ford, could not only talk money and how he made it, but could also tell a lot about the old West. Some said he was really as rich as Conrad.) But Conrad had one great distinction—the Conrad herd of buffalo, the second biggest in the world. He must have felt some interest in the animals to keep them on his range land all those years.

Senator Paris Gibson, who founded Great Falls, was still alive but it was a long time before I met him.

More important than these because we saw him every day was Charlie's neighbor in the same block, old Mr. Albert Trigg, and his wife Margaret, whom Nancy called Mother, and his daughter Josephine, Nancy's best friend, the assistant librarian at the Public Library. Trigg, short and fat and with a big head, had a sense of humor and used to quote from a mythical book, *Leona Leota, The Prairie Flower,* and I still remember the words in which he signified that he had talked enough and was going home, "So saying, he darted into the thicket and was lost to view."

And Trigg would get up, put on his hat, and walk out.

Younger than Trigg, more contemporary with Charlie, were George Calvert the contractor and Bill Leard who ran the steam laundry. Leard was bald-headed and determined to cure it and though he wore a fur coat and big fur mittens and ear-muffs he went without a hat all winter; in those days nobody, not even Indians, went without hats.

"Winter out here," said Charlie, "will grow hair on a gum-boot," and sure enough Leard's bald poll was covered with a thin white fuzz which didn't look so much like hair as like frost coming out. Did you ever see the frost come out on a brick wall? That's exactly how his head looked, but he called it hair and was comforted.

Then there were the Wilgur brothers, big land-owners, who in their day had been men of violence. It was said—but there was no proof—that they had got some of their land by killing. Todd, the eldest, was afraid to die, and people knew this and it was really cruel the way they treated him. As soon as Todd came into a saloon, someone was sure to say, "I hear old man so-and-so has cashed in," and they would all begin talking about how many old-timers had died lately, and keep it up, till Todd, not saying anything, would give them an ugly look, hating them, and drink up his likker and get out. He knew what they were doing. They deliberately spoiled his drink. Instead of giving him a lift, it let him down; he felt worse than he did before.

Of course, Todd had been a bad one.

Younger still there was Percy Raban, the newspaper man, who looked like a slim blonde Briton and wanted to write child stories; and Olaf Seltzer, foreman in the machine shop and making big money, but discontented because he wanted to be an artist. He would work at his easel a while and then get discouraged and quit. Years later I suddenly saw his paintings on 57th Street, New York and recognized the coloring even before I stooped close enough to see the name.

Then there were the smelter crowd who lived across the river on Smelter Hill, graduates of Boston Tech; but these we saw only at dances, and they, of course, were western only in the same way I was—we all wore Stetson hats. Stetson hats were indeed, for the younger generation, almost the only sign still left of the old West. Except for Charlie and a few hangers-on around the livery stables, nobody wore boots.

Charlie In Montana

But there were, as yet, none of the professional westerners you see nowadays, people in tremendous gauntlets—Charlie never wore gauntlets in his life—and red or purple shirts and enormous hats. They didn't talk like such gentry do either—for instance, I never heard the word cow-poke till I came to New York. It reflects, of course, on modern beef cattle—specially bred monstrosities with hulking bodies and almost no legs. In Charlie's day you didn't need to poke beef cattle, the long-horns were as active as deer; the problem was to catch up with them.

Then there was Walter X, a spender and an all-round sportsman, who imported a whole pack of expensive Russian wolfhounds, savage brutes and big and ugly, and Walter was warned they were dangerous. He built them a special kennel on his ranch at the edge of the badlands, and allowed nobody to feed them except himself and his daughter, a little girl twelve years old. He made her go into the kennel with him every morning. At first he had to carry a club or a pitchfork, but in time the dogs got used to him.

The baying of the pack and their howling at the moon—apparently the prairie moon made them homesick—scared all the game out of the neighborhood, but Walter was proud of their ferocity—their almost brainless ferocity—and told many stories about them. He was afraid, he said, that the dogs would die of insomnia, because they not only kept each other awake by howling all night—a nice noise if you like it, but most people don't—but also they didn't dare lie down; they had to sleep standing up. The instant one lay down to take a snooze his brothers and sisters would conclude that he was sick and they'd all pile on him and tear him apart. Walter lost several this way.

"But that," he always concluded, "is what you need in a wolfhound."

Walter, something of a wolf himself—a blonde wolf (he was quite nice looking and a fancy dresser)—at last decided that the pack was ready and invited his friends to a real European wolf hunt with horse and hound. The guests were forbidden to bring rifles but they all had six-shooters.

They scared up a big dog wolf at the edge of the badlands and the whole pack began baying and belling—you could hear them for miles. The hounds showed speed but no judgment. Instead of staying bunched up they trailed out across the flat, the fastest first, and left the riders behind and ran the wolf down—they ran him down all right, they could run faster than he—but they came up to him one by one. And though the wolf was slower on the run he was quicker at turning; he dodged them again and again. At the last instant the wolf would whirl, and the hound, redeyed and crazy with excitement, would run right past, unable to stop.

When this had happened half a dozen times, the wolf, terrified at first, got back his nerve. The next time the hound came at him he just jumped aside and then jumped back again—and struck.

A wolf doesn't bite like a dog; he strikes with his jaws just as you'd strike with a hatchet. He jumps in, strikes, and jumps away, the two jumps being so quick that they seem all one movement.

That's what the wolf did now. As the hound hurled past, he jumped in and struck, and tore the hound's foreleg almost out of the shoulder. And a hound with only three legs is not much good.

The wolf did this repeatedly. The hounds caught up with him one by one; and one by one he slashed them and jumped away. He had crippled four of them before the riders got close enough to shoot. Then he ducked into a coulie.

Walter had to stand a lot of razzing, but he could take it.

According to his account, after four or five hunts like this—the only wolves they got were the ones they shot—the wolves would actually come down to the ranch at night and crap on the back step and race around outside the kennel and invite the hounds to come hunting. They'd travel miles and miles panting with urgency, said Walter, just to crap on the step. This sounds improbable. Of course, the wolf *has* got a nasty laugh—did you ever see him grin? No wonder his base-born and servile cousin, the dog, doesn't like him.

People praise dogs all the time for loyalty but when you come down to cases the dog is really a traitor—he betrays his own people. He helps his bully, Man, to kill his own kindred, the wolves and coyotes and foxes.

Finally came the night when Walter got drunk and stayed in town. Next morning early his daughter went out to feed the hounds, as she had done every day since they came. Fortunately it was cold weather with a fierce wind blowing and she had on a fur cap and coat and big mittens and a muffler around her throat, and over her shoes a pair of her father's boots.

She started to feed the hounds and one of them snapped at her, and instantly the whole pack jumped her. Knocked her down and piled on her and began to tear her apart— that's what they do with any game: tear it apart with their teeth.

Her clothes saved her from being killed but they had her stripped almost naked before the men could run in with clubs and pitchforks and beat them off. It was a long time before the kid got over it.

Walter came home about noon and the foreman told him and asked what he was going to do.

"I'll show you what I'm going to do," said Walter, and he got the Winchester and went out in the corral and shot the whole pack.

Catch a wolf young enough and you can tame him same as a dog. Which, no doubt, is how dogs began. The

Husky or Malamoot, the Alaskan sled-dog, is still very close to the wolf, and so is the purple-tongued Chow, the meat-dog, which the Chinese breed to eat.

There was a rancher outside Great Falls—I forget his name—who killed a bitch wolf and kept one of the pups and raised it on a bottle, and the pup, growing up and not remembering his mother, probably didn't know he was a wolf. Once, just before I came to Great Falls, the rancher brought him to town.

There was also a bulldog named Napoleon, a sort of four-legged barfly who didn't belong to anyone in particular but hung out around the saloons and patrolled Central Avenue, the business street of the town; and this Nap was a killer, he had killed several dogs. Most dogs fight but seldom actually kill the loser. The bulldog, the collie, and the German police dog do kill—they never show any mercy.

When the wolf came down Central Avenue, Nap saw him, or smelled him, and started across the street to run him away. Men standing in front of the saloon called to the rancher and warned him to watch out, but he seemed to think the wolf could watch out for himself.

Nap came waddling across the avenue, snarling and slobbering, telling the world that he didn't like wolves and what he was going to do about it; and the wolf stood on the curb—not saying anything—and watched him. He had never seen a bulldog before and perhaps didn't know what it was. It smelled like dog, but, as far as he knew, no dog ever looked like that.

The bulldog *is* a queer looking thing with his bandy legs and his head so big it hides the rest of his body. Approaching, end on, he must have looked to the wolf like a mask with two bow legs. A very ugly, dangerous sort of mask—deadly even.

"Look out!" yelled the men. "If Nap gets hold of that wolf he won't let go."

The wolf, however, didn't intend to be got hold of. As Nap came within ten feet of the curb, the wolf—who hadn't said a word, Nap did all the talking—suddenly jumped, not at him, but slantways across in front—perhaps playing, perhaps just to see what would happen. Nap reached for him and snapped his jaws, but missed. That clarified things. The next time the wolf jumped—jumped in and jumped out so quickly it seemed all one bounce—he popped *his* jaws but didn't try to hold on—just slashed and jumped away. And behold, the entire front part of Napoleon's face, his snout and big upper lip was dangling down in ribbons, dangling and bleeding, bleeding and spurting. That ended the battle. The wolf stood there, sort of laughing, ready to play some more, but Nap was not as stupid as he looked. He didn't know exactly what had happened but he knew he didn't want it to happen again. He stopped snarling and went back, fast, to the saloon; and though they stuck his face together with adhesive and patched him up the best they could they had to change his name and call him Rags because that's the way he looked. When I saw him, months later, he still had the scars. He looked at you through up and down seams as though through the ribs of a grating.

When Charlie chose he could tell this story in a way that would make a dog-lover grind his teeth. For Charlie was sometimes perverse, and anyhow his animal affections were for horses. Even after all these years he still had a faint prejudice against dogs because of the sheep who drove out the cattle. I don't mean that Charlie disliked dogs, or any other animal; he just liked horses so much better that there was no comparison.

Great Falls was a compendium of the surrounding country, its history and people, and had I had the wit, or a philosophic guide to point it out to me, I could have seen right there traces and vestiges of the five strata, the five historical layers of the West: (1) the halfbreeds, hunters, trappers, prospectors, and the early railroaders who killed off the buffalo; (2) the cattle barons and the civil war soldiery who rounded up the Indians on reservations; (3) the sheepherders who drove out the cattle; (4) the nesters who drove out the sheep; and now, in my day, the fifth or permanent layer, the bankers, money lenders and real estate men who took over the nesters.

And there, right across the river, built in gigantic steps up the gorge of the Missouri, harnessing and taming the wild Upper Falls and dominating the whole countryside with its Big Stack, was the copper smelter with its hierarchy of officials and technical people on Smelter Hill, and its laborers, "Austrians," i.e., European peasants, in Little Chicago. Peasants with such outlandish names that the foreman, putting them to work, would say, "Hell, I can't remember that—I'll call you Jones." The big red "Rustlers Card" which you filled out when you applied for work, had at the top a blank line: "Your name———", and under that a second line: "Your real name———".

Great Falls was a metropolis. It had not only the smelter and lesser business enterprises but two newspapers, *The Tribune* and *The Leader*, owned by the same man, printed on the same press, and to a considerable extent edited by the same talent, but bitterly and ranquorously opposed in politics, one Democratic, the other Republican. There were no other political groups. Nobody in Montana had ever heard of Marx but we did hear about the Wobblies, the I-Won't-Workers, and hated them ferociously. I hadn't the faintest idea what they wanted. I just knew they were wicked and un-American—*everybody* knew that.

14

Charlie And Sundry Survivors From
A Gaudier Day

The frontier had long been declared closed. There was no more open range, the prairie had been fenced from Texas right up to the Canadian Line, but Great Falls still had a few characters from cattle days.

One of Charlie's favorites was the stuttering old-timer, Py-anner Jim, who played the piano at the honkytonk dance hall saloon. According to Charlie, Jim and his wife Nellie were the originators of a joke which has been circling the world ever since. Jim came into the Silver Dollar with a brand new black eye and said Nellie had hit him with the alarm clock. Bill Rance, the proprietor, asked, "Was the clock going?" Jim: "It was gu-gu-gu-*go*ing when it hit me!"

Jim and Nellie did not get along very well. As Jim expressed it, "When we gu-gu-*go* to bed at night I take the wu-wu-wu-*Win*chester an' Nellie takes the axe!"

Once they were camping up in the foothills and had a quarrel, Jim hiding in an old prospector's shack and Nellie down by the crick. This time *she* had the Winchester and began pumping it into the cabin.

"She cu-cu-cu-*could*n't see me," said Jim, "but by gu-gu-*God* she seemed to know just where I was. I got down flu-flu-flu-*flat* on the floor an' the bullets were tearin' up splinters a yu-yu-*yard* long all aroun' me. Then I got up on the cu-cu-cu-*cross* beam under the roof an' right off she began shu-shu-shu-*shoot*ing thru the shingles—she made 'em fly!" (Only he called them "shakes." Homemade shingles, you know, split off from a block of cedar with a shake-knife. You can lie in bed and look up and see the stars shining right through a shake roof, but the grooves in the cedar run water down it like a gutter, and as long as you keep the roof clean no rain comes through. Of course it's only back in the timber—which means up in the hills—that you can get shakes: no shingles out on the prairie.)

Jim drank and Nellie beat hell out of him every so often, but she wouldn't let anybody else do it. When he got in trouble—as, in spite of a mild and friendly disposition, he frequently did—Nellie always either rescued or avenged him.

One gentleman, a newcomer to the Falls, got warlike in his cups and was going to kick Jim's teeth in. Jim held him off, exclaiming, "Wu-wu-wu-*wait* a minute, stranger, did you ever su-su-su-*see* Nellie?"

Nellie heard of the fracas and stopped past the butcher's to borrow a cleaver—or, as we say in Montana, to borrow the loan of a cleaver—and in half a minute she had every man in the house trying to hide under the grand piano. It must have looked like a surrealist picture—Impotence Seeking Solace in Music.

Long afterward, Irvin Cobb told what he called Charlie Russell's best story about Py-anner Jim. Jim and Nellie retired and built a cabin on Flathead Lake, and Jim, who loved pumpkin pie, planted pumpkins. He grew a beautiful vine which spread all over the place but nothing came of it—nary a pumpkin. A dirt-farmer told Jim what was wrong. "That's a female vine—you've got to get you a male to fertilize it."

But Jim drew the line. "I've been a no-good low-life all my days, but du-du-du-*damn*ed if I'm going to start pu-pu-pu-*pimp*ing for a punkin!"

Nancy Cooper Russell

Charlie Russell and Niece Isabel
in Indian Costume at Lake McDonald

From left to right: Skookum, Charlie Russell, Austin Russell, Minnie Hume and Nancy Russell, on cabin porch at Lake McDonald.

Pen and Ink — 1898

Pen and Ink — 1900

I dont think that 1820 looks worse than 1920
If fine fethers make fine birds   Why should we decorate
our selvs in the plumeage of a buzzard   This funiral garb
covers, few of our blemishes   the ouley way to hide bow legs is
go to bed

A wish is but a beggars gift
   Tho if fary wands were mine
Id turn the land all happiness
   And give to thee and mine

Chas M. Russell

Charlie's Personal Christmas Card

"Parthian Soldier"
Made by Charlie for Austin (1911)

"Painting the Town" from Pen Sketches by Chas. M. Russell, The Cowboy Artist.

(*W. C. Ridgley Printing Company, Great Falls, Montana*)

"The Shell Game"

Charlie And Sundry Survivors From A Gaudier Day

People might look down on Py-anner Jim but everyone had great respect for Nellie, even the honkytonk girls, tempestuous pieces who when they got drunk fought like tigers among themselves. Their favorite weapon was to knock the rounded rim off a tall mixed-drink glass and then jab it—like an apple-corer—at the rival beauty's face. Several of them carried a ring of scars around the muzzle where some other girl had been quicker on the jab.

Not that it was the policy of the house to have the girls get drunk too early in the evening. They were supposed to take "chippy drinks," silver-fizz or golden-fizz, while the gentlemen, drinking real drinks, got polluted. The Zero, that invention of the Arabs, gives "power" to all numbers—add it to 1 and it becomes 10. The presence of ladies made all drinks a dollar. In the crib houses even beer—a nickel anywhere else—cost a dollar a bottle.

Jews were few and far between out west but Great Falls had two, Werner and Jacobs, brothers-in-law and rivals in the clothing business. Werner was an attractive person with a sense of humor. Jacobs had none—a big, solemn, owlish looking fellow—but his store was the bigger and the better stocked, and he was prominent in the Chamber of Commerce, the Townsite Company, the Boosters Club and so forth.

One day the Werner boy came home crying—the kids at school called him Christ-killer.

Said he earnestly, looking up at his father, "Poppa, did *we* kill Christ?"

"No, son," said Werner, "that was Jacobs."

Of course, the Werner kids told their Jacobs cousins, and Jacobs senior said indignantly to Charlie, "That little Jew's going around telling people that *I* killed Christ!"

"Oh well," said Charlie, the comforter, "hardly anybody believes it."

129

CHARLIE RUSSELL, *Cowboy Artist*

One of Charlie's most intimate friends was the old time freighter Johnny Matheson—which, he told me, means Son of the Bear—a big, raw-boned, heavy-jawed Scotch Canadian, who had lived this side the line for forty years but was still intensely British. "Just go to England once," Charlie kept telling him—Charlie had been there, "and you'll come back a howling democrat."

But John didn't believe it. He was ten times as English as the king.

Put out of business by the railroad—people, even loyal old-timers, won't ship freight by wagon-train when they can ship by rail—a Scotch friend had grub-staked John to a dry land ranch outside Great Falls where he grew wheat, and though he didn't like farming he preferred it to driving a team at the smelter.

He was an old bachelor, afraid of girls, the respectable ones, and though whenever John came to town Charlie had him stay overnight he wouldn't come to supper if there were going to be any women except Nancy. One of her girl friends, Kitty Conan, set out to kid John, and one afternoon in the big living room she actually got him to talking.

John told a story about an old prospector up in the Crazy Mountains and how a couple of boys from a camp down the creek kept breaking into his cabin and stealing molasses. One day, just at sundown, he came home, found the door open and heard a noise inside. Carefully leaving gun and knife outside, lest he be tempted to use them, he rushed in, banged the door to behind him, dropped the bar into place and shouted, "Now I've got you!"

Only to discover when he struck a light, that what he had got was a momma grizzly and her four cubs: and momma, cornered, was strictly on the warpath. And *him* inside with no knife!

"Was he scared?" Kitty asked.

130

"Scared? He was struck fartless. Oooh *God!*" said John with an agonized howl, suddenly remembering he was talking to a lady, "I knew I'd say something—I *knew* it!" and he lit out for the ranch and wasn't seen in town again for weeks.

You figure him out on the high prairie, alone in his one-room shack, writhing in anguish over the horrible word he had used in front of a girl.

And he was six foot two and powerfully built and had a jaw that came right out of the stone age—he would have looked good in kilts.

John, though always a bachelor, had not always been so backward about ladies. I remember his telling a trip he made with his freight wagons. A cowpuncher who had gone broke in town went with him and brought along a lady friend who also wanted to change her luck by trying another city. I think they were going to Sand Coulee or some such metropolis.

"It made me sore," said John, "that she hadn't come with me instead of with him. Well, we camped that night up along the river, and when I turned loose the horses they scared up a jack rabbit an' he jumped into the little bedwagon at the back an' I cornered him an' caught him by the ears. The other two had made their bed up alongside the front wagon an' I was still sore about the girl so when they weren't looking I reached down inside the puncher's blankets and tucked the rabbit in way down at the foot.

"The jack lay quiet in the warm dark—as completely cowed as you would be if some angel or something suddenly snatched you up by the ears an' shut you in a dark place such as you had never heard of or imagined.

"Well, we had supper, an' the girl went to bed first. As soon as she stuck her bare legs down inside the blankets, the jack, terrified, began to kick, an' clawed her with his toe nails from hip to ankle.

131

"God! what a yell she let out an' came busting from the blankets—she thought it was a grizzly bear at least.

"The jack came out with her and took off across country for Canada, thirty foot to the jump. I bet he passed the Arctic Circle before he stopped to look back. Other people might like bare legs in bed, but not him. He hoped to God he'd never feel another leg.

"The girl ran to me for protection an' I washed her wounds off with whiskey an' alkali water, an' put her in *my* bed—she wouldn't have a thing to do with the puncher; she thought he done it on purpose. *He* was sore as a boil—but not at me—he couldn't figger out how in hell the rabbit got there. The girl stayed with me the rest of the trip. She said she'd seen punchers with gray-backs (cooties) an' even with crabs, but he was the first she ever met who had rabbits.

"*He* never heard the end of it. When they saw him coming down the row, the hookers used to say, 'Make him take off his pants before he comes in—there's no knowing what he's got in 'em.'

"So when he went calling on ladies he had to carry his pants over one arm to show it wasn't his night to have rabbits."

◄§ 15 §►

Great Falls Background

Py-anner Jim and his fellows fitted perfectly into the mosaic of Charlie's background, but these quaint survivors from a dying age were soon shoved aside by other and more modern figures—the people I met at work.

I had washed street cars about a month when one autumn evening with a full moon riding in splendor over the prairie we went out to a dance at Black Eagle Park. There I met some of the Smelter people and especially the Chief Sampler, Arthur Crowfoot, a poker-faced Briton, who danced with Nancy and asked if I was going to stay in Great Falls. She said yes, and he offered to put me to work the next afternoon. I would be in the Sample Department and the pay was three dollars for an eight-hour day— big money then. It was also change-shift and a seven-day week, for the smelter never shuts down. You can't bank a blast furnace while you take a holiday.

In the smelter everybody wore thick leather mitts—not gloves—big and loose so you could yank them off quick with your teeth if you got some hot slag inside; and upstairs, where they charged the furnaces with coke and limerock and copper ore and briquettes, you wore a handerchief around your neck and in it a wet sponge to pull up over your face to breathe through. The wet sponge made your face sore and the flue-dust, floating in the air, got into your pores and made enormous pimples. Everybody should have worn goggles, but in those days they made no attempt to

133

protect the men, with the result that quite a few of the old-timers had only one eye. Everybody had the smelter cough and hawked and spat continually.

That first afternoon shift, four to midnight, I thought I was in hell. I had never seen such a place. The noise, the smoke, the strangling sulphur smell, the flue-dust clouds floating like dark ghosts down the dark gangways, the sudden rivers of fire from unexpected outlets; the vast "tapping floor" fading off into blackness at either end, the blast furnaces like a row of tall brick houses, each with a stream of molten slag pouring out at the bottom; the reverberatories, and opposite them the battery of converters—bottle-shaped furnaces like pot-bellied siege guns which suddenly keeled over at an angle and coughed and threw flames to the roof. And all the time rolling back and forth overhead—rolling and roaring and thundering—two huge traveling cranes trailing ladles full of molten "matte" which spat and splashed and ran over and dripped on the floor. And each splash, played over with flame, kept on spitting and splashing like a miniature volcano. Yes, it really looked like hell, a more horrifying hell than Dore's Dante because it was mechanical.

Johnny Mulberry, blase to all this—*he* wanted to be a railroader—broke me in and showed me how to take samples every time they tapped a furnace; and later we went upstairs to the "feeding floor" where they charged the furnaces—here instead of traveling cranes was a miniature railway—and we went back into a specially dark and sulphurous alleyway among the McDougals, the roasting furnaces, and stood at last on a shaky square of dirty wooden flooring, and Johnny, coughing and spitting, yanked on a cable and behold, the floor became an elevator and rose, swaying, up through the darkness past the "High Line"—a full-sized railroad—and the enormous ore-bins and took us up right to the smelter roof, acres of roof shelving off into dimness; and we smelt fresh air and beheld God's sky, and miles away, and as blue as paint on the moonlight, the Little Belt Mountains.

I used to go up there at least once every night just to look at the mountains.

Charlie had a real horror of the smelter and always refused to visit it. And he was right: what it stood for meant the end of everything he knew and loved.

One of his friends, the old-time freighter John Matheson, went out to the smelter to take a job as a teamster. It was day work, the pay better than ours and the teamsters had Sunday off, but John took one look and said No. He'd rather work twelve hours on a wheat ranch—and yet he hated ranching. Said he to Charlie, "I knew that if I stayed in that place—that noise, that smoke, that machinery—I'd hate it so that I'd die."

He too was right.

Right alongside the smelter and shut off from it by heavy fire-doors is the Concentrator Mill. Both are built in set-back floors, like steps, up the gorge of the Missouri.

Quitting my job in the smelter and starting to work in the concentrator was like graduating from a fiery and roaring hell into a cool, wet, dripping, and murmuring purgatory.

In the smelter everything is done by fire; in the concentrator by water. The smelter moves its stuff in hand trucks and trams and lorries and traveling cranes and ladles and miniature railways. The concentrator moves its stuff by water and gravity; everything flows downhill. At the top are the crude-ore bins and the crushers, at the bottom the tail-race.

In the smelter it is all fire and bitter dust and biting smoke; most things are too hot to touch, and some things— the converters—explode like siege guns. In the concentrator everything jumps and jiggles and drips and gurgles; when

135

the rest of the mill is quiet, just purring and murmuring, the bucket-elevators, lifting their intolerable load, suddenly groan like lost souls.

I liked the concentrator better than the smelter though I had to work much harder. I had not only to make rounds of the whole west mill but also to drain the automatic sample-boxes—some as big as coffins—dry the residue on big dryer tables, scrape it up and roll it with an iron rolling-pin, pulverize it, screen it, and put it through the dividers, and cut it in half, and cut it in half, and cut it in half till there was just enough left to fill a sample can.

The sampler's job had the enormous advantage that the only dry, warm, and comfortable place in the whole mill was around the big dryer tables; and there, on night shift, I was king and didn't take orders from anyone, not even from the concentrator foreman. The foremen, consequently, didn't like us—regarded us as spies—and so did the men, because we were always checking up on the tonnage they put through. If there came a howl from the main office they knew our samples started it.

Wherefore it was frequently remarked about our boss, the Chief Sampler, "Oh, he's English and he sticks his belly out!"

For the smelter was full of Englishmen come down across the Line to work in the States. Some had helped build the smelter twenty years before, but still stayed English and still despised America. There were also a large number of Bostonians, mining students from Boston School of Technology —Technical Bostards, the smeltermen called them—and they despised both the English and the Americans.

One technical youth, a sampler, roused the ire of the English straw-boss by asking for a lawntren.

"You damn fool," said the Briton, "we don't say lawntren, we say *lan*-tern!"

"Ah well," said the Bostard, "it is notorious that the lower clawss English cawn't speak their own language."

Then he wondered why the English didn't like him.

In the sample department I worked off and on with four Britons, Harry Rudge, Billy Priest, Willie Wilson and Alec Strangways—the last two regular picture Englishmen, little blonde mustache and all.

Wilson was a foundling, as he expressed it "born under a hedge," and the foundling home had farmed him out to a school where they raised jockeys. The way you raise a jockey is not to feed him. Catch him young, starve him and stunt him. In spite of starvation Wilson grew too tall and the school turned him out. Knowing nothing except how to ride he joined the cavalry, the Prince of Tech's regiment, and served in the Boer war and later in India. Afterward he went to Canada and joined the Northwest Mounted.

Wilson told me—and I retailed it to Charlie—that the English cavalry recruit has to ride bareback for six months before he can use a saddle.

Which made Charlie snort. "And I suppose," said he, "that in the navy they make the recruit swim for six months before he can board a ship. A man who has any serious riding to do and does it bareback is certainly a fool."

"You told me yourself," I reminded him, "that Indians generally ditched their saddles when they went into battle."

"That's different," said Charlie.

Concentrator life had its idyllic moments. Sometimes, past midnight, down the wet and slumbrous aisles of whirring and pouring machinery you would hear Pan's pipes or get a fleeting glimpse of fauns and satyrs. American satyrs.

One morning just at dawn—and summer dawn comes early in Montana—I was making my rounds and crossed over the High Line—a narrow plank walk right up under the roof with the floor and its murmuring vanners sixty feet below—and heard, overhead, a queer thumping, a rhythmical thumping. Parts of the concentrator were full of thumping machinery, the Huntington mills, for instance, and the crusher jaws—crunch, crunch, crunch, thump! But the crushers and the mills were at the far end of the building, blocks away, and this noise overhead, whatever it might be, was not mechanical.

I went up in the nearest elevator shack and looked out over the roof, acres of gently sloping roof descending in steps down the gorge of the Missouri.

There, perched on a projecting gutter and swinging his heels was Palagi, playing his mouth-organ, and before him MacLoughlin, a big, tall, gangling kid, tap-dancing, or, as they called it then, clog-dancing. They grinned when I appeared and looked a little bit foolish but went right on. The dance was called, so they told me, "Give her a hug every morning."

Then there was the time at dead of night when Billy Wilson and I came single file across another runway and saw far down below a circle of flickering arc-light and in it Mat Cooper, another big, tall, skinny, long-legged kid—he was stage-struck, wanted to go on the Orpheum Circuit—dancing all alone, dancing like mad to imaginary music and for an imaginary audience. To whom, when the dance was done, he swept off his cap, chalk-white with copper-slime, and bowed again and again right to the floor.

It was goofy but it was charming and I would have stayed quiet till the end but Bill was a crass materialist. He tiptoed over to the nearest light-bulb and screwed it out of its socket and hurled it down on the iron top of the drying table, where it burst like a bomb and scared Mat out of his dream.

He was shouting mad for a minute, then he grabbed his torch and yard-long sampler's pipe and came to look for us, and he knew all the runways and ladders and cellars just as well as we did.

The other two Britons, Harry Rudge and Billy Priest, palled around together, and Priest was supposed to be responsible for the "Valentine" nuisance—intensely personal effusions with mixed-up tenses, short on meter but long on insult, which the weary sampler, already sore with the prospect of two weeks' nightshift, would find floating in the coffee compartment of his lunchbucket. There are few things more irritating than to find a soggy, indelible-penciled poem soaking in the coffee on which you have been depending to give you a lift.

In my valentine I didn't like the last two lines: but Palagi's—in dialect—was of such a nature that he didn't like *any* of the lines.

Palagi, thinking it over, took his Valentine so much to heart that he lay in wait in the deepest sub-cellar, down by the ghostly white torrent of the tail-race, and caught first Harry and then Bill, *privatim et seriatim,* and beat hell out of both of them. He staged a reign of terror for three nights, the two Britons lurking in the sampler's shack, afraid to come out, and sending me forth, like Noah's dove, with olive branches, till the Superintendent horned in and threatened to can all three of them. He said he didn't mind a few fights down by the tail-race but he wasn't going to have the whole mill turned into a circus and samplers with flaming torches chasing each other down every gangway.

There was an ambiguous personage, the Cellar Rat, a wordless European of unknown race, who lurked down in the sub-cellar all the time to keep the launders clear. You would be bending over, draining a sample box, and out of the corner of your eye you would catch the gleam of a torch, not yours, and there, down a long colonnade of piling and stooped like a gnome, would be the Cellar Rat watching you. As soon as you turned to look at him he went away.

Gnomes, fauns, satyrs, three European figures, all in one smelter! Outside the smelter there were also nymphs, not so European. Going home at midnight, Scotty, one of the samplers, got off the smelter car at the same corner I did, but he had to walk much farther. After he left me he passed a grocery store and there on the sloping top of the big bread box was a colored gal who accosted him, "Ain't you going to love me?"

"No, I ain't going to love you!" and Scotty went on, simmering pleasantly with self-righteous indignation until at the second crossing a new notion occurred to him — maybe it was free!

He turned and hurried back but the bird had flown; the top of the bread-box was empty.

This doesn't seem to have much to do with Charlie except that it's part of the background against which I see him. A fading tapestry; but a tapestry with depth and sound effects — yes, with touch and taste and smell.

Even now a whiff of sulphur brings back the smelter and the McDougal roasting furnaces, tall sheet-iron towers with six superimposed floors, or hearths, of variegated flame, each floor a different hue. Gasping for breath through a wet sponge; stooping, bent double, to look through the furnace door, you saw a mysterious something moving toward you — a revolving rake sweeping round and round — and the roasting concentrate falling in fiery snow to the floor beneath. It was like a view of a ploughed field in hell — but the furrows were smouldering, red, blue, and gold — and raining down on them in sudden gusts and whirlwinds that fiery snow.

It's very discouraging because now that I stop to think of it this book is not a picture of Charlie as he really was but of Charlie seen through my eyes and against *my* background, not his. The trouble is that I don't know what Charlie's background was — his mental background, that is. How did the world look to him? In all the years I lived there, I never once tried to learn what he was thinking.

Wholly preoccupied with my own affairs, I went around in a daze, astonished at the things which happened to me — very ordinary things, all of them — and paying no attention to anyone else except as they impinged on sacred Me. The result is that my memory of Charlie is mostly gaps and blanks: a tapestry full of holes.

Charlie had been to Europe and seen real medieval tapestries, and didn't care for them — "the drawing is feeble, the colors ugly, and the composition awful." He didn't care much for Egyptian carvings either but liked some of their figures in the round and expressed surprise at two pictured heads I showed him — a young pharaoh's melancholy smile and the famous head of Queen Tye. "That's a really beautiful woman," he said. (She, distinctly, didn't have a meaty nose.) He liked the Assyrian lion hunts, and felt contempt for the horses on the Parthenon — "No horse ever looked like that."

For Charlie was a philistine of the first water: most of the old masters made him tired. When his wife dragged him to Paris he inspected the galleries one morning and refused to go back — once was *a*-nough. "Who in hell wants to look at miles and miles of entombments and descents from the Cross and martyrs crucified upside down — I'd just as soon visit the morgue. They must have been a miserable bunch, those artists."

I repeated what we heard in High School. "The artist didn't have much choice; he painted what he was paid to paint. His patrons, popes and princes and rich men afraid of hell's fire, were trying to buy their way into heaven with a holy picture. If the artist liked birds or animals or soldiers or whatnot he had to put them in the background."

"Maybe that's true," said Charlie, "I noticed right away that the background was often the best part of the picture, the only interesting part."

Charlie was just as crude about modern art. He admired Church's *Heart of the Andes*. (So do I, but I gather that if you like that sort of thing it puts you at the bottom of the class.) He disliked Whistler but often quoted his famous equation, "The critic is to the artist as the flea is to the dog; the flea lives off the dog but he doesn't do the dog any good."

However Charlie didn't act on this principle. As soon as he went east and met other artists his work showed that he accepted their criticism and thereby greatly improved his own pictures, especially in composition and in weeding out unnecessary detail. His early work is inferior in color, in plan, in every way, to what he produced after he had been criticized — sometimes politely, sometimes not — by other artists. Criticism, by people who know, *does* help.

Being a philistine of the first water has its advantages — Charlie kept his integrity. If he didn't like Scandihoovian art he said so, and it didn't matter how many authorities told him he ought to admire it.

Sometimes his untrained judgments seem to have been good. For instance, he didn't think much of Michelangelo's famous murals but did like his sculpture. Years afterward I read somewhere that Michelangelo agreed with him: he painted under protest because the Pope compelled him; what he wanted to do was sculpt.

Charlie did not read much fiction. He liked Rex Beach — he had met the villain of *The Spoilers* — and Jack London, and the *Wolfville* stories, but he cared little for most two-gun westerns. *The Virginian* offended him; he didn't like the hanging of the hero's best friend, Trampas' faked-up song

("Why didn't he *sing* a real range-song?") and such details as the hero riding the same horse all the time, riding hard day and night and never once changing horses.

He wouldn't read the historical novels of the period but one day he picked up Stanley Weyman's *Under The Red Robe* and the first words were "Marked cards!" and Charlie read it through and liked it. Nancy read *Quo Vadis* aloud and it gave Charlie such a prejudice against the Romans that he would never admit they were anything except a bunch of dirty murderers, "sitting around on marble bleachers torturing prisoners!"

Mentally Montana was a slough, a "by-u" or backwater cut off not only from the life-giving sea but even from the river, the sluggish, erratic mud-river of American culture. We knew nothing whatever of what went on in the world.

Europe was visibly preparing for the cataclysm of the First World War — Montana took no interest and couldn't be bothered.

Contending schools of art were turning Europe upside down — we didn't know it, though we *had* heard about Cubism and the *Nude Descending a Staircase*. The other western artists who visited Charlie all made great fun of the *Nude*.

And all this was infectious; even the Boston Tech people, who presumably had done some reading at home, lost the habit as soon as they came west, and settled down very comfortably to playing poker, and, a little later, bridge. Most of them married local girls and that put the ki-bosh on books.

This does not mean that *I* repined about the surrounding ignorance. I didn't know we were ignorant. I just thought the Westerners were crude and used worse English — meaning un-St. Louis English — than we did at home.

That we inhabited an intellectual vacuum never occurred to me.

When you consider Charlie's environment you wonder that he ever produced anything except the crudest kind of comics. What was there to encourage his art? Nothing whatever. Charlie is a proof that a man on a desert island will produce art if he has it in him.

Charlie often got orders for pictures he couldn't — or wouldn't — paint.

When the Russian Doukhobors, the "Old Believers," a fanatical religious sect who have big colonies up in Canada, got the notion, as they do at intervals, that the Resurrection was at hand, they shed their clothes and started out naked across the prairie to meet the Redeemer. An enterprising American photographed it and came on a high lope to Great Falls to have Charlie paint a picture.

None of the nudes, even the young ones, were particularly alluring and there were too many middleaged and elderly people with whiskers and wild hairs and warts, and too many pregnant women. Even I could see that these photos were just plain nasty.

"We can make a lot of money," said the entrepreneur.

"We're more apt to go to jail," said Charlie, "and anyhow that's not the kind of picture I want to paint."

Then there was the millionaire mining man, Tom (King) Cole, who ordered a painting of Buffalo Bill and the Grand Duke Alexis on their celebrated buffalo hunt. When the painting was delivered, King Cole rejected it. Charlie had shown Buffalo Bill shooting a calf and that wouldn't do at all — he must shoot a bull. Also the bull, running for his life, must not have his mouth open and his tongue out. King Cole's bulls must die in the high Roman way with their mouths shut. He and Nancy had quite a correspondence about it but Nancy won. She had learned

144

by experience that before you start to paint a picture on order there must first be a cash deposit.

Why? Because the buyer tells you what he wants but he isn't able to make you see it *his* way. You paint it *your* way, and he's sure to be disappointed.

⋘ 16 ⋙

Domestic Details

When I went to Montana, Charlie and Nancy already had a steady income from a calendar picture contract renewed every three years with either the Osborne Company or Brown & Bigelow, the two biggest calendar companies in the world. This gave them enough to live on and made them feel safer than most artists; anything else they sold counted as profit.

Nancy was a spender. Charlie was not, but he was tapped pretty steadily by people out of luck. He wouldn't stake anybody for gambling. Though he could play poker he never did when I knew him — very few artists are card players — but in later years Nancy occasionally played bridge.

Though a spender, even a lavish one, Nancy was canny. She could, and did, save money and invest it. They owned, and rented out, a cottage on the street behind them, Fifth Avenue North; they had a small dry land wheat ranch a few miles out of town near Johnny Matheson's place; and Charlie was part owner of Con Price's ranch on Kicking Horse Creek up in the Sweetgrass Country. They also had stock in the local cemetery which, for some fool reason, struck me as funny — the idea of investing in a cemetery!

They lived only a couple of blocks from the edge of town; then came a long gap, a mile or more, and then a suburb called Boston Heights.

146

Their frame house, though small by St. Louis standards, was ample for their needs. On the ground floor were a minute storm vestibule, a big living room, a big square hall, dining room, bathroom, kitchen, a small bedroom for the cook and a closed-in back porch for the icebox. Upstairs there were three bedrooms, another bathroom — an afterthought, without a tub — a trunk room and a hall with a cot which could be used as an extra room. I remember that one winter three Episcopalian clergymen were snowed in with us by a blizzard for the best part of a week. And, of course, there was the big log studio with two cots where Joe DeYong and I "batched" when Charlie and Nancy went east. We cooked on the big iron heating stove.

The house had a wide yard — three city lots — in the back a corral, a two-horse stable with a hayloft, a chicken house, and, later, a garage. When at last Nancy got a car, Charlie refused to drive it. They didn't use the car in winter; they put it up on stilts.

Beside transient guests, they usually had somebody living with them. The Indian girl, Jo Thorpe, stayed with them while she went through high school. Kitty Conan, Irish, was with them off and on for years. Later Charlie and Nancy went to California and brought back Nancy's half sister, Ella Allen, and put her through high school and business school. When I went to Great Falls she was working for the *Tribune*. She married a big Englishman, Frank Ironside, and Charlie's cousin, Ferg Mead, called her Mrs. Stonehenge because that sounded even more English than Ironside.

In the morning Charlie woke up and got up very soon after sunrise. So soon, in fact, that in summer — when the northern sun rises very early indeed — his wife would lie in bed holding her breath, knowing that if she stirred a toe Charlie would wake. It took him only a couple of minutes to dress and then he went down and watered and fed Nee-*nah* and the chickens and got breakfast for the whole family — hot cakes and bacon and coffee, boiled coffee of such authority that you needed only one cup.

Sometimes they had a cook, sometimes not, depending on whether Nancy was feeling ladylike or economical; and it was a real shock to a new cook to wake on her first morning and crawl painfully out of bed and find that the gentleman of the house had her breakfast ready. But it was a shock to which they soon accommodated themselves. No cook ever left Charlie's roof except to get married. One married a fireman and tried to break him into getting breakfast but he wouldn't break, his argument being, "After all I ain't no artist."

Immediately after breakfast Charlie went out to the big log cabin studio in the side yard and painted till noon. He did surprisingly little fumbling around waiting for inspiration — he went right to work. About once an hour he sat back and rolled a cigarette and looked at what he had done. Usually he turned his back on the canvas and sat with one knee over the other, studying his work in a hand mirror that always lay on the shelf under the window. The mirror, of course, reversed the picture and showed up any bad drawing. This is such a common practice among artists that you'd think anybody would see what he was doing, but lots of people didn't. One woman reported that Charlie Russell was the most conceited man she'd ever met. "He *is* fine looking, you know," she said, "but goodness, the way he admires himself! Almost all the time we were talking to him he sat there with his knees crossed looking at himself in a mirror. He hardly condescended to look at us. He'd puff at his cigarette and then twist the mirror around a little and admire himself some more. You never saw a girl so shameless about it."

Evidently Charlie was having trouble with the picture: "fighting it," as he called it. That's why he usually worked on two or three canvases at a time — when one didn't satisfy him he'd let it dry and work on the other. Then, when he went back to the first, he saw right away what was wrong.

At noon Charlie stopped work and went into the bathroom and washed his brushes with ivory soap. He washed each brush slowly, carefully, completely, until it was entirely clean. Never, no matter what happened, did he leave the house till he had washed each brush. He bought the best brushes and treated them right and they lasted a long time.

You'd naturally expect an artist to be slapdash, untidy and careless about mechanical details, but Charlie wasn't. No jeweler could have been more painstaking with his tools. And, as remarked above, he never sat around waiting to be inspired. He went to work — and inspiration came.

When he finished with his brushes lunch was ready. If it wasn't, Charlie sat down at the table and — talking — ate all the cookies but one; and then was apologetic, "Oh Mameso, I've eaten almost all the cookies!"

This annoyed Mameso — also me, if I was there; I wanted in on the cookies. But I was at a disadvantage; I had been brought up St. Louis fashion to eat my cookies last. Charlie was like a horse: the horse eats the oats first and then the hay. If there were cookies on the table Charlie ate them first; then he didn't want much lunch.

After lunch Charlie rolled a cigarette and strolled out to the cabin and lay down on the couch and went to sleep right away. He slept half an hour and then got up and rummaged around to see if there was any candy. Though he had stopped drinking long ago, he still had the ex-drinker's taste for sweets. He ate four or five pieces and then put on his hat and hitched up his sash and went downtown and divided the afternoon between the Silver Dollar, the Mint, and one of the cigar stores. He bought drinks with everybody but drank Vichy water. At five o'clock he came home. He was as punctual as if he worked in an office and watched the clock.

After he had fed and watered Nee-*nah* and shut the chicken house, Charlie sat at the long table in the living room and looked at the paper till suppertime, reading mostly the local items, especially anything about old-timers. Supper was the big meal of the day—the big event of the whole day for me. I loved to cuddle up to the table, and—as Charlie expressed it—eat till I fell over backward. Of course, he was exaggerating.

Charlie himself was not a heavy eater: he ate what he liked and as much as he liked but he practically never over-ate. In all the years I lived there I never knew him to be sick at the tummy but once. That was on a trip to Missoula when circumstances forced him to eat two enormous turkey dinners in swift succession at two different houses. The second dinner was too much. The host and hostess were almost strangers; Charlie didn't like to ask for the bathroom; with sudden sweat bursting from his forehead he excused himself to smoke a cigarette and went out in the yard and ran around like a chicken looking for cover. There wasn't any cover. Nancy became alarmed and followed him. The whole thing was very painful.

Nancy, on the other hand, got car-sick every time she went on the train. The menu on the diner tempted her to folly. She fell; and like produced like as before. But *she* called it sick headache.

I too had my misfortunes. When Percy Raban, the tall, blond, British-looking reporter who wanted to write children's stories, got married he and his bride wound up their honeymoon at Charlie's camp in the mountains, and we all went back together to Great Falls. The train was late; we were stranded for hours at Belton; the lunch counter had closed, there was nothing to eat, but somebody had given Nancy an enormous box of candy-coated almonds beautifully colored, red and blue and pink and peppermint green and chocolate, and licorice black, and white and yellow, and we ate them all, which is to say I ate most. When at last the train came it was crowded. Percy and his wife had to share a lower berth and I had the upper above them. As soon as I got down, the almonds got up. I spent the entire night climbing in and out of the berth—which was restful for Percy and family—and spoiled a brand new white sweater; it was colored all down the front like an Easter egg and it never washed out. Charlie was entirely unsympathetic: "I *told* you not to eat more than a bucketful."

Life is full of humiliations. Charlie's best friend and neighbor, old Mr. Trigg, of sturdy build with a big intelligent-looking head and short arms and legs, was also, when life got too much for him, somewhat short-tempered. One of Charlie's favorite stories was how Trigg—knowing by experience what was coming—sent his wife and daughter out of the house so he could express himself freely while putting up the stove pipe. An ordeal which darkened every autumn. This time the pipe was even more than usually recalcitrant; the last section—the climactical, critical, all-important last section—simply refused to be fitted. Trigg had cleaned it beforehand but now as soon as he slid one end into place the other slid out and covered him with soot. Trigg paused and expressed himself several times but it didn't do any good.

Finally on the verge, the ultimate edge, of apoplexy, he groaned and dashed out into the street and stopped a passer-by, a perfect stranger, and asked if he knew how to fix a stove pipe.

"Well, I'll try," said the stranger, who—like Dom Manuel—would try anything once, and he went in and reached up, two-handed, and fitted the length of pipe—just as Trigg had done twenty times over—and jiggled it, and with a comforting little click both ends slid into place.

"There you are!" said the stranger, straightening down again and dusting his hands. He expected to be thanked.

Trigg glared at him half a minute and then exploded, "Why you dirty blank blank blankety blank, what do you mean by coming into *my* house and doing it like that!" and he gnashed his teeth and ran the interloper off the place.

I don't know whether this is a true story or not but I know just how Trigg felt. I too have gone shambling and fumble-fingered all my life through a world inhabited exclusively by efficient, effective and adequate interlopers.

A Summer At Lake McDonald

The summer of 1910 I was late leaving the smelter and when I got up to the Lake, I found my kid sister there, her second trip west—a West which was an even bigger eye-opener to her than it had been to me.

The Russells had other guests that summer but the only one I remembered was the New York animal painter Philip R. Goodwin, a slim, black-haired, very boyish looking fellow —he was about twenty-eight but didn't show it—and I was surprised—after some of Charlie's other friends—to find so well known an artist so modest.

Goodwin had studied with the famous Howard Pyle and usually spent his summers in the Maine woods or up in Canada, his specialty being calendar pictures, moose hunts, bear hunts and so forth for Remington Arms. He also painted big circus posters for Barnum and Ringling Brothers and had just illustrated Teddy Roosevelt's book on African hunting. This had been an anxious job as Teddy paced off every shot and remembered just exactly how he stood; and he snarled and made faces and skinned his teeth to show how the lion looked. Goodwin wanted to put both man and beast in the foreground of the picture, but Teddy was adamant, he had killed at one hundred and fifty yards and one hundred and fifty yards it had to be and not a hair's breadth less. And at one hundred and fifty yards either Teddy or lion—whichever was in the background—looked very small.

That summer Charlie too had an aggravating job—pen illustrations for an enormous book by the wife of an early railroader. While her husband was surveying and building the transcontinental line the old lady had gone with him, riding thousands of miles by stage and horseback, and had seen many interesting things—for instance, temporary wooden rails covered with rawhide and coyotes gnawing the hide and spitting out the splinters—and she too, like Teddy, knew just exactly what kind of pictures she wanted. There was an argument which went on for days about the frontispiece. She wanted a fancy picture of herself and Pal (her husband) as bride and groom with wedding bells and streamers and hovering cupids. Amorini, she called 'em. You know, the nasty bloated little things with rosy buttocks who look as if they were made out of bubble gum. Charlie drew the line at amorini. After much anxious talk with Nancy he submitted a sketch of Pal on horseback escaping from a howling mob of Indians, halfbreeds, bandits, vigilantes, hold-up men and crooked gamblers, only to be run down and roped by Cupid —in chaps—on a pinto pony.

"Oh no!" said the lady, "that won't do. Pal *never* ran away from anybody!"

"Well," said Charlie, "if he wouldn't run away from a bunch like that—!" He left the sentence unfinished but the implication was clear: anybody who wouldn't run from that bunch ought to have his head examined.

To supervise the job, the authoress stayed at one of Apgar's cabins at the foot of the Lake and the first time she saw Goodwin he was working on a model yacht. It was Goodwin who showed Charlie how to stretch a rubber band from the tiller to the mainsail so that the ship would steer itself and come about in the wind. She thought Goodwin a mere child and when, next day, she saw him making oil sketches of the river mouth—to be used later in calendar pictures—she expressed admiration as you would to a child and referred to the sketches as "pretties."

Goodwin, as a practicing artist, was indignant.

Charlie never forgot it. Every few mornings he'd ask, "Well, Philip, going to make any pretties today?"

Charlie himself made two square rigged models, shrouds and all, with a lookout at the masthead and a man at the wheel, but they were slower than Goodwin's yacht and did not come about as neatly.

This was Goodwin's second visit to Lake McDonald. He had been there the year Charlie built the big new hearth and chimney, and the two of them had decorated the fireplace by scratching the wet cement with drawings of moose, deer and so forth.

Outside the cabin, under the bottom log, Apgar put a wide strip of concrete to run off the drip from the eaves—it's always the bottom log that rots first—and Charlie marked it with big bear tracks which he knew how to make with the heel and ball of his hand, his thumb and the tip of his fingers. This was years before Hollywood started the fad of recording the stars' footprints; in fact, it was years before Hollywood.

Beside these memorials Nancy had made a set of white cotton screens—intended primarily for dressing rooms when the whole bunch bunked in one cabin—and every guest who stayed overnight had to write his or her name in india ink, one leaf of the screen for each summer.

The chimney of brick and stone and cement caused a catastrophe. Apgar had built it around a wooden form, and when it had set and Charlie and Goodwin took over, some bright person suggested that the quickest way to get the form out was to burn it. It was quick all right.

This has a faintly medieval flavor. When Perceval, God's fool, came from the forest where his mother had brought him up in ignorance of the world, and saw his first knight, and killed him, he wanted the armor but didn't know how to take it off, so he built a fire to burn the dead man out. When Sir Gawain, horrified, protested at such a barbarous proceeding, Perceval explained himself:

"My own modir telled me,
When the dart should broken be,
Out of the iron, burn the tree."

In other words, burn the broken wooden shaft out of the iron spearhead, which was indeed the only way to get it out in an age when there were no corks and therefore no corkscrews. So Perceval was going to burn the dead knight out of his armor.

But when Charlie and Goodwin started to burn out the chimney they almost burnt out Montana. Within three minutes it was roaring like a blast furnace with a flame forty feet high shooting out the top. They were scared sick, afraid of starting a forest fire. When they tried to cut off the draft with a wet tarpy across the fireplace the suction pulled it right up the chimney. They stayed up almost all night before the damn thing burned out. The chimney was cracked from bottom to top and had to be pointed up. The moral is—before you start something you can't stop, consult an engineer. But you can't expect an artist to know everything.

Forest fire is an ever present danger in the mountains. Even the ground, the floor of pine needles, will burn. Started by vandals, by careless campers, by locomotives, by lightning, it goes with the wind; it burns uphill quickly and downhill slowly; it will jump fire-guards and rivers and even lakes. More than once we went up to Belton with fire burning on either side of the right of way and railroad guards every few hundred feet.

A Summer At Lake McDonald

The summer Goodwin was out there, the sky was hidden for weeks. You could look straight at the weird red sun; soot fell in a black snow storm day and night; the lake was covered with scum.

The wind was blowing our way and one evening, just at sunset, the fire came up over the crest of the foothills across the lake. We went down to the shore to watch. It was a solemn, terrifying business. We'd see the flame reach a pine tree a hundred feet high and run right up it to the top. We thought the whole country was going to be ruined and Charlie talked about breaking camp and getting out before the fire reached Apgar and cut us off from Belton. But that night the wind changed. The fire went back over the hill and the lake was saved. Finally it rained; the lake and the river cleaned themselves and danger was gone for that summer.

The pine woods are a great place to fall in love, and Goodwin, as was inevitable, went suddenly soft at the top about kid sister. Big brother was dum, as big brothers are, and it wasn't till I was out in the canoe with Aunt Nancy and remarked on Goodwin's queer clumsiness—as if he was mentally slipping off the perch—that she explained what was happening. I began to laugh in a nasty way and would certainly have made trouble, but the steerslady forestalled me, "One snicker out of you—just one—and you go back to town on the evening train!"

I knew my Aunt Nancy and there were no snickers.

Kid sister was too young and Goodwin too unenterprising for anything to come of it, but no doubt it enchanted the whole summer for both of them. *El Encantado* the enchanted man—and the enchanting maiden.

Goodwin was bashful; he couldn't sing in the daylight, but one night, just after Nancy blew out the light, he surprised us all by suddenly piping up in a high-pitched, unnatural, embarassed but resolute voice, and sang an ancient ditty from his childhood. I remember it now: I was lying on my back looking up at a star through a crack in the shakes, and suddenly out of the dark, like a thin fountain of light—thin but with a crystal clearness to it—that jet of song.

Not a very romantic song, you will say, but artists in love express themselves in queer ways,

> "My father had an old black horse
> With a pain down in his thorax,
> So he took a great long rubber tube
> And filled it full of borax.
> He put one end in the horse's mouth,
> In his he took the other;
> When he blew in that horse blew out
> And the blow almost killed father."

I suppose it stemmed from New England; we had none of us heard it before and it made a great impression. Especially on Nancy, who sang it next day and not knowing what thorax means she transposed the syllables so that it came out—with a pain down in his throw-ax. Depth-psychology being then unheard of, we just thought it funny.

Nancy often did transpositions with words. In New York she and Charlie had seen a play about Beau Brummel and one day in camp when I looked particularly disreputable she told me to go shave and called me Bro Bummel. Kid sister pounced on that with a shriek and for the rest of the summer addressed me as Bro. Warmed with Goodwin's approval, she was getting quite cocky and beginning to show off. Which was hard on me but the rest didn't seem to object. Charlie even encouraged her.

Here is her picture in squaw dress and Charlie in the black wig Nancy bought him. The picture is poorly posed as it makes Charlie look much shorter than he was. I don't know what the jagged, surrealist-looking thing is in the foreground—something out of the Unconscious of the forest?

Speaking of shaving, Charlie had an unfair advantage: his whiskers were so light that he shaved only every other day, and in a pinch he could always cheat—rub talcum powder on his chin and look as if he had just come from the barber.

Late in September, with the geese going south, the tourists already gone, and the muskrats building their winter homes, we broke camp. Nancy, Josephine Trigg, the cook, and I returned to Great Falls, but Charlie and Goodwin went up to Con Price's ranch in the Sweet Grass Hills at the head of Kicking Horse Creek.

Charlie had known Con ever since they punched cows on Milk River and in the Basin, and they were partners. Charlie put up most of the money but Con ran the ranch and did the work. According to Charlie's biographers, Adams and Britzman, the partnership lasted five years—I had supposed it lasted longer—beginning January 1, 1906, and Con sold the ranch, brands and all, in 1911. They had three registered brands: their cattle brand was the Lazy K Y (⋉), and two horse brands, the 3, and the ∃ and T.

Nee-*nah*, his Indian pony, was getting old and sway backed, so Charlie picked two young range horses, Dave and Sun-Dance; and he and Goodwin rode them back to Great Falls, stopping overnight at ranch houses—a five days' ride, every inch of it in a lane between wire fences.

Sun-Dance was a beauty, a yellow horse with white stockings and a cream-colored mane and tail. Dave was a red bay with a black, very thick double mane which hung down on both sides his neck. He, though hard-mouthed— you had to be always reining him in—was reliable; Sun-

Dance was not. But this didn't appear till they got to town and had to stand all day in the corral.

Born on the range, neither horse had ever seen an automobile or a train, and when they drew near the Great Northern tracks, Charlie warned Goodwin to keep his horse's head up and be ready to pull leather and hang onto the horn. A drag of empties was going by, rattling over the joints of the rails, and the two horses, pricking their ears and sniffing with curiosity, walked right up and almost put their noses on the moving box cars. They showed no fear at all. (And yet Nee-*nah*, who had lived in town for years, almost threw me when a piece of newspaper blew across the street.)

Dave loved to run—and he lathered up like a barber. When you ran him, his chest—and your thighs—would be covered with long slathers of yellow foam, and every so often he tossed his head and threw more foam back across your face. He was rough riding—you could feel every pound of his hoofs—but he wasn't ugly or vicious.

Sun-Dance, the picture horse, was meant for Nancy— she had an expensive saddle and a headstall with silver conchos—but after a few days of standing in corral, he developed an ugly trick of raring up on his hind legs as soon as you forked him. Raring up is the most dangerous thing a horse can do—much more dangerous than bucking—because he is liable to over-balance and fall backwards and drive the steel saddle horn right through you. When I took him out to exercise him—we had to run both of them every day or they got too wild—Charlie would hold Sun-Dance's head till I got on and then walk him down the alley. After he had walked a few yards he was safe but Charlie was afraid to let Nancy ride him and got rid of him. He got rid of Dave too: he said he wasn't running a racing stable and it wasn't fair to a young horse to keep him cooped up in a corral in town.

A Summer At Lake McDonald

These were Charlie's last horses, though Nee-*nah*, sway-backed and with a big belly, was still alive and active when I left Montana. That would be 1917, just before the First World War, and Nee-*nah* died not long after.

Charlie And The Indians

A dog cannot see color: his world is like a photograph, all blacks and grays. He lives largely in terms of smell. Scent takes the place of color; the air brings him a forever flowing, forever changing harmony of scents and smells and savours and stinks and stenches. He seems to find very few flavors offensive.

As the tourists sits and shades his eyes and admires the view, just so the dog sits and twitches his nostrils and reads the wind. It may be much better reading than a newspaper.

As the dog sees everything in terms of smell, Charlie saw everything in terms of form and color. Their harmonies took the place of music.

They also, apparently, took the place of morals. For Charlie professed no morals, and yet, when I knew him, he led a highly moral life. But perhaps what worked him was not morality but just kindness.

Charlie was forty-six in 1910: high time to take stock and find out whether he was really going anywhere or just getting older.

As far as I know he never did take stock, so we'll do it for him.

Had he changed at all except to put on weight and get heavy—heavy, not fat—and middleaged looking?

Outwardly, yes. He had stopped gambling. He had stopped drinking. He began life as a professional hunter; he had now stopped killing. Though he still went deer hunting

162

with Frank Linderman and Bill Kreighoff and other people, he did not carry a gun—he had reached the point where he didn't like to kill.

For the same reason he had stopped fishing.

Fishermen laughed at this, citing the well-known fact that the fish is cold-blooded and has no nerves and can't feel pain.

"Sure," said Charlie, "that's why he jumps six feet out of the water when he gets the barb in his eye. And the live-bait minnow, wiggling on the hook, wiggles because it tickles him. And the caught fish, slowly drowning with a rope through his gills, really enjoys it."

All which is sissified stuff and completely contemptible to any red-blooded he-person. Also to lots of ladies. Charlie cocked a cold and cynical eye at the church-going, Jesus-loving ladies who wear fur and feathers.

"Oh, women don't think about things like that!" But Charlie was foolish enough to believe that a woman who really loved Jesus would think about it.

Differing from our hair-on-the-tummy writers, both male and female, he was horrified by his only Mexican bull-fight. Once was a-nough—he never went again. When they first tortured the bull with banderillas and then crowded the poor old bag-of-bones horse up on the horns to have his guts torn out, Charlie didn't like it. He very much didn't like it—and said so.

His hosts urged him to go to the next fight—a very special one, the biggest of the whole year. All the government people would be there, and the church dignitaries, both male and female, and the English and American colonies, and the Europeans. *Every*body would be there.

"Everybody but me and Mameso," said Charlie. This was a big disappointment to Nancy, but she knew better than to overstep the line. She wept but she stayed away.

It is convincing proof of Charlie's strength of character and his grim look that he was able to get by with all this mollycoddle stuff—no gambling, no drinking, no killing and torturing just for sport. Lots of people, big important people, were offended by his attitude, but nobody dared look under his brows and say so.

Yet Charlie was no reformer. He never interfered with people's drinking. He divided every afternoon between the Silver Dollar and the Mint and the cigar stores which at that time were just fronts for gambling. He kept all his drinking and gambling friends and the others with more highly scented vices, and the smell didn't seem to bother him.

A bad smell doesn't bother a dog, you know, he sniffs and appraises each and all impartially. He likes to go out in the street and roll on dead fish and other things which you and I don't care for. Evidently to the dog any smell is a good smell and the stronger the better.

Artists are that way too. To them everything is form and color; and morals, if any, have nothing to do with it. I think Charlie's only moral was not to cause pain.

Yes, Charlie had changed in both his work and his mind. As was shown by the change in emphasis of his later pictures. He still painted violent action—gun fights, bear hunts, bucking broncos and so forth; but these were painted to sell. The ones he really liked were more contemplative: the tribe—women, children, old people—on the trail of the buffalo runners: riders in the snow or at a waterhole: Indians singing the sun down. The sweep is wider; the country, though less detailed, and the sky, play more part in the picture.

Charlie had not changed his mind about the Indians. He knew their faults and how stubborn they are, but he also knew how badly we have treated them.

Said he, "If you ever went out on a frozen river and sawed ice all day with the wind screaming over the edge of the bank, you'd know why that's *one* job the white man is willing to give the Indian.

"He won't give him any other. The white man kills off the buffalo, takes the Indians' land, deprives him of his only means of livelihood, refuses to hire him as a ranch hand, and then tells you that all Indians are lazy—a bunch of stinking gypsies!"

They have become exiles in their own country.

The Cree tribe were even worse off than the rest because they were legal exiles. They used to live in Canada but got mixed up with the French halfbreed rebellion led by Louie Riel, and for fear of the Red Coats, the Northwest Mounted Police, they fled south across the Line and hid in Montana. The Great White Father in Washington let them stay but wouldn't put them on a reservation because they were officially Canadian. And the Canucks wouldn't let them go back.

When I was in Great Falls a dying remnant of the tribe led by Chief Little Bear wintered across the river and made a few dollars peddling moccasins, beadwork pouches, and hideous monstrosities called hatracks made of "buffalo horns" (really cow horns picked up on the range) set in a profusion of cheap red plush and brass tacks. You can't imagine anything less Indian-looking: as far as art is concerned they really *have* become gypsies.

Knowing by experience that kids do better at peddling such stuff than grown-ups, the bucks stayed out of sight, with the result that a little Cree girl, ten years old, was lured into a saloon and ganged, and the white gentlemen went around telling what they did to her. They regarded it as a joke, and so, apparently, did the authorities. Nobody was arrested. When three or four people talked as if they might make trouble the gentlemen involved hauled tail and left town. Nothing was ever done about it.

The Crees knew better than to do anything—they had been getting that sort of treatment ever since the Star of Empire started west.

That winter the church ladies got together and staged a big charity bazaar—*not* for the benefit of the Indians—and the chief attraction was an amateur opera called Little Almond Eyes, the name of the heroine. The scene was laid in China and the whole thing was a sort of Chinese *Mikado*.

Charlie's wife was the mainspring. She worked, as she always did, like seventeen tigers to make it a cyclone success. She was determined to take in twice as much money as they ever did before.

She always rang Charlie in on anything like that, and one of her publicity stunts was to hornswoggle the local printer into stamping out, gratis, hundreds of little yellow cardboard figures about three inches high with a string through them to hang on your lapel. She had everybody in Great Falls wearing them, and the conductors, brakies and so forth on the Great Northern.

These figures were blank, no printing on them, and Charlie's part was to ink in Little Almond Eye's face and clothes. He drew the first few quite carefully, but when he saw boxes and boxes of the damn things, he rung *me* in—doubling the output but diminishing the art—and we put in our evenings for a week drawing Little Almond Eyes. One result being that Charlie, who had often remarked my enthusiasm at table, called me Little Gormondize.

The show *was* a cyclonic success, the take being four times as big as before; and when they had attended to the local poor, Nancy—still by virtue of sheer driving force the executive—spent the surplus on blankets and food for the Crees, starving, freezing, and dying of pneumonia across the river. The church ladies objected—but failed to make their objection stick—and one, a very pious sister, said indignantly,

Charlie And The Indians

"I wouldn't have worked half so hard if I'd known we were going to waste the money on a lot of dirty old Indians!"

When Nancy repeated this at supper, Charlie went on the warpath, declaring he'd like to see *her* —the pious lady —in a tent out on the flat with not enough food to keep warm, but presently he calmed down and philosophized it, "I suppose she's never in her life been really cold, or really hungry, and she hasn't enough imagination to guess what a tent's like in winter."

He excused all sorts of things in other people on the ground that they just lacked imagination. *They* didn't see everything in images as he or any other artist did.

Genealogical Research

Along about this time a maiden lady distantly related to us inherited six hundred dollars and decided to look up her ancestors. Investing it in Chicago—can't imagine why Chicago but she certainly got plenty for her money—she discovered that she, and by assumption *we* (I did most of the assuming), descended by way of sundry bastardies from the Plantagenet kings of England.

The first Plantagenet, you remember, was Henry Short-Shanks—but Charlie called him Duck-legs—father of Richard the Lion-hearted, the lion part deriving from the way he roared for help whenever somebody chased him up a tree. Richard went around Europe insulting people, and the insulted ones always defeated him in battle and chased him up a tree. He spent a considerable part of his reign in jail.

Later there was a second Richard, who died in jail impaled on a red hot poker. (There's one for the whodunit writers—a red hot poker, internally applied, leaves no external scar.) But the third was Crooked Neck Dick, who, after strangling both his nephews in the Tower, fell sword in hand at Bosworth Field, the last of a fighting family.

"Fighting?" said Charlie. "It seems to be mostly murdering! I'd just as soon descend from Jack the Ripper."

Descent from the Plantagenets implies descent from most of the other dynasties, but *my* favorite ancestor was the Emperor Isaac Angelos of Constantinople, one of the Byzantine rulers. He is unique. Plenty of monarchs have waded through blood to royalty but Isaac is the only emperor who ever *cried* himself onto a throne.

Because he was related to the royal family, the reigning tyrant, Andronikos, condemned Isaac to death. Ike, the most unwilling of martyrs, fled for sanctuary to the great cathedral of Saint Sophia, where he stayed safe all afternoon, holding onto the horns of the altar and weeping. A crowd collected, staring at first, then weeping in sympathy—Andronikos having made himself odious to everybody—and on toward evening the crowd grew into a mob and suddenly boiled over and went roaring up the street to the palace and dragged the tyrant from his throne and lynched him.

In the confusion some nimble-witted Greek caught up the crown and put it on Isaac's head. Our ancestor, still in a pea-green panic, suddenly found himself emperor.

This would make a good end to the story but Isaac, crowned, turned out to be as objectionable as Andronikos; the Crusaders came thundering down on their way to the Holy Land and laid siege to Constantinople; and Isaac, having made a mess of everything, was cast into prison and strangled by one of his cousins, a gentleman called Eyebrows —I'm not inventing, look it up in Gibbon—who succeeded him on the throne, and came, in turn, to a smash finish by being thrown off a tower.

The Crusaders did the throwing. Nice people, all of them, especially the Crusaders, who claimed to be working for Jesus. They had set out to liberate Jerusalem from the heathen and ended up by looting Christian Constantinople.

All of which I retailed to Charlie with embellishments.

Charlie, knowing me, took it with considerable salt and was not unduly elated; but his wife, having no ancestors to speak of, was much annoyed by our imperial descent.

"But, Mameso," Charlie soothed her, "just think how fast we've descended. And anyhow, if we met them on the

street, I don't suppose that Richard the Runt, and Louie the
Lump, and Henry the Hippopotamus would speak to us—
they'd pass us up like a couple of bad smells. And as for
Crying Ike of Constantinople, I think the kid invented him."

Charlie took the flat-footed stand that no emperor had
ever been named Isaac. Ever had been or ever would be.
Ike the Kike he called him and refused to believe in his
existence.

So Nancy forgave Charlie but not me. She developed
a habit of remarking in my presence, "After all *I'm* only
common clay."

Which was indeed fairly evident.

I regret to add in the interests of veracity that this
royal and imperial descent proved to be a mistake. It applied, if at all, to an entirely different branch of the family
and Charlie had no tainted blood. But it was nice to talk
about while it lasted.

Charlie, of course, would not have talked about it even
had it been true. He did singularly little boasting of any
kind. I never heard him tell a story or incident in which he
figured in a heroic way, nor did he ever claim to have fought
Indians, prevented a lynching or anything like that. He was
modest even about his many years on the range, saying,
"I was just a common rider. Most of the time I was night
wrangling. I was never a champion roper or a bronco buster
—when I rode a bad horse it was because I couldn't get a
good one."

According to Tommy Tucker's book, Charlie was not
always just a common rider. When he went as a "Rep"
(representative) of the Judith Basin outfits he was paid
an extra ten dollars a month. And in those days ten dollars
was a lot more money than it is now.

Tommy is inclined to high romance (he has Charlie
rescuing maidens, killing Indians, hanging halfbreeds and

Chinamen—I hope the movies have not got hold of Tommy) but the Adams and Britzman biography confirms the "Rep" part, saying Charlie and Kay Lowry were sent as "Reps" to the Moccasin roundup by the Judith Basin outfits. "Reps" could read all brands, and they worked with the regular crew, cutting out and holding in a separate herd the calves of the outfits they "repped" for.

Charlie never told about this in my hearing but then he was that way too about his art; he never bragged. Commonly he called himself an illustrator. However, he offset this by saying that a good illustrator was just as good as any other artist. And an illustrator has to be able to draw—some artists can't.

20

Horses Of Humiliation

You must not suppose that Charlie associated only with old-timers and localites. His home was a place of pilgrimage for any actors, writers, people of that kind who passed through Great Falls, and especially for the new generation of western painters of whom I remember only Gollings, Ed Borein, Maynard Dixon, Olaf Seltzer, and—much later—Joe DeYong.

Once the Chicago sculptor Lorado Taft, who was making a cross-country lecture tour, came to dinner and surprised us by looking and talking exactly like an artist in an English novel. I had seen his *Solitude of Soul* at the St. Louis World's Fair—if I keep mentioning the Fair you must remember that it was *the* cultural event of the Middle West though not quite as devastating in its effect as the earlier Chicago Fair, which, so they say, put European handcuffs on a whole generation of American architects—and I prompted Nancy to speak of it, and she made an even bigger hit with Taft than Charlie did. When she was fixed up she was so pretty that she didn't need to say anything very original to make a hit with artists. This last sentence sounds faintly disparaging. As a matter of fact, Nancy was not only pretty; she had—quite apart from her good looks—just as much personal charm as Charlie. It wasn't only artists who fell for her.

Taft's companion, an eastern university man chock full of culture, stayed overnight—the sculptor being booked elsewhere—and talked, very interestingly too, about modern art, till Charlie, suddenly bored with the rarefied conversation, announced, "Well, you people can sit up as late as you like but this is Saturday night and *I'm* going to take a bath if it chokes the sewer."

Which naturally annoyed Nancy.

Charlie often said things like that just to shock people. He also, out of mere perversity, often put on an act and made himself look much more ignorant than he was.

Once up in the Rockies, Charlie, Nancy, little Mary (the cook), and I were alone in camp—I don't remember why there were no guests—and quite late at night just as the girls were going to bed, we heard a voice high up on the hill, hollering for help. It was a hoofer, i.e., a tourist who walked through Glacier Park instead of hiring a horse, and he had got benighted on the trail and lost his way and was badly frightened—the night woods *are* frightening, dead silent by day but full of mysterious sneaking-up-on-you noises as soon as it gets dark—and just as he was getting really panic-struck, he saw the lights of the cabin far below, but didn't, for fear of cliffs, dare climb down.

Charlie and I took the lantern and rescued him.

He saw Charlie's sash and boots; Charlie and I needed haircuts; the girls in braids and barefoot with slickers instead of bathrobes over their nightgowns—no pyjamas then— all these circumstances, combined with Charlie's vocabulary to mislead him. He thought we were backwoodsmen, Montana equivalents of Ozark hillbillies. Charlie and Nancy played up to him. He never suspected that they went every winter to New York and had sold pictures in London; and when at last I rowed him across the foot of the Lake to Apgar's he promised to send us all the illustrated Sunday papers.

173

But this was at Lake McDonald and we were talking about Great Falls.

The guests who most impressed me were the eastern artists, Marchand, Krieghoff, Goodwin, Joe Schuerlie, Jack Young-Hunter and others who came, one or two at a time, to spend the summer with Charlie.

First of them was Marchand. When the Russells had met him in New York he had been an aggressive, loud-talking fellow; but now, when I saw him, he was slowly dying—he didn't know it but his wife did. The Reaper's shadow was already over him and had changed his whole nature. He had become the gentlest, friendliest, most appealing person you ever saw.

His wife, a Hungarian, was a beauty. She had been a chorus girl, and Marsh, dubious about marrying what he called a broiler, had taken her and the Russells out to dinner and asked Charlie afterwards what he thought about her. Charlie's answer was sententious: "Pretty as a painted wagon and sound as a hound's tooth."

Which Marsh told the girl when they were married and evidently she had never forgotten, for now, years later, she repeated it to me, laughing a little as if it was foolish of her to remember such a thing but you could see she thought it important.

"Then said Tua, Turak's daughter, 'Short words to him, he spoke without thought: long words, life-lasting, to me.'"

Perhaps they had helped keep her as sound as a hound's tooth.

Marsh had an interesting experience with one of Charlie's friends, a big ranch owner from Montana who was in New York and Charlie introduced them. They hit it off very well together and several days later the rancher went down to Marsh's place on Broadway and Fortieth, a studio building full of artists, and found Marsh, who was illustrating some magazine story, painting from a model, not nude. Marsh introduced the girl and they talked a while and then Marsh was called downstairs to the phone. He was gone some time and when he came up again he heard a terrific row inside the studio.

The rancher, assuming all models were tarts, had propositioned the girl; when she said no, he grabbed her and started to undress her by force. Marsh had to get help from next door and actually pry the gentleman off. He told Charlie, "If you've got any more friends like this, don't bring 'em around."

Then there was another New York artist, Bill Krieghoff and his wife Julie. Bill had a perverted sense of humor. He was quite short—Charlie called him Duck-legs—and wore a derby hat and he would pull it down till his ears stuck out flat and hump up his shoulders and walk along Fifth Avenue, mumbling to himself, busy as all hell counting on his fingers. Julie, a dressy little person, couldn't stand this; she'd hurry on ahead and act like she didn't know him, and Bill would trot along right behind her, still busy counting. He'd have everybody watching them. More than once a cop asked Julie if that man was annoying her. As she didn't want to bail him out, she had to explain, "It's my husband, dammit!"

And the cop would look sympathetic and back off.

The Russells had been quite fond of Julie in New York, but when she came to Great Falls, what a difference! She never got as far as the mountains; life in a prairie village bored her sick. Her one idea was to go downtown and have a happy thought—the then New York expression for a drink. It was a real relief to everybody when at the week's end she had a real happy thought and went back to New York. Bill stayed and went up to the mountains.

He wanted to paint portraits but was then making a living, quite a good one, as a commercial artist for Dick

Outcault, the Buster Brown man, who was the first to have a whole office full of artists and sign their stuff and syndicate it.

On Outcault's staff there was a foreign artist whom Bill greatly admired and he told how this foreigner and his son went chippy-chasing together. Charlie didn't like the idea. Said he, "If I ever started into a whorehouse and met my father coming out I'd feel so uncomfortable that I'd go home —I wouldn't want to do anything that evening."

Bill was disgusted. "You're not a cowboy, you're a puritan. I'm ashamed of you!"

"That's the way I feel about it," said Charlie. "When I'm getting my ashes hauled I don't want the family along."

One of the old-timers who used to come to the studio and argue with the "foreign," i.e., New York artists, had a wife, a big fat lady with a large family, a sense of humor, and a laugh that was really worth hearing. The other ladies, not having a sense of humor, objected to her laugh, with the natural result that when her name came up at table, Charlie would remark, "I believe I could learn to love her."

Which, no matter how often he said it, always annoyed Nancy, and Charlie would have to smooth her down, "Now, Mameso—"

The fat lady had been a widow when she married the old-timer and he a widower; both of them had children before and after. One of the stock jokes of Great Falls was that the old-timer came home and asked, "What's all that noise out in the yard?"

"It's been that way all afternoon," said his wife. "Your children and my children are picking on our children."

"Well, I'm going to take a plank to 'em!" said the old-timer and he went out and planked the bunch. You could hear them all over town; it sounded like Custer at the Little Big Horn.

This same old-timer told Bill Krieghoff and me the story of Charlie's saloon.

Charlie was lavish with his money, an easy victim for a hard luck story, but he would not stake anybody who wanted to gamble—he had been trimmed too often himself when he was young at Faro and Stud and Three Card Monte.

One year at the end of the season when they had just been paid off, a puncher turned up with a pitiful tale of his brother's family on the point of starvation, and Charlie came across generously. The puncher, who had no starving brother, went straight to the nearest gambling emporium and rang all the bells, he almost cleaned up the place. Whereupon, being an honorable person, he proposed to divide, Even-Steven, but Charlie would take only what he had given. "Have it your way," said the lucky man, "but from now on me and you are partners."

"Sure," said Charlie, having heard that kind of talk for years, and he thought nothing more of it; but late that night, when he was slightly drunk, he suddenly learned that he and his partner, the lucky man, were now proprietors of a small saloon, a plank shack, at the edge of town. His partner had bought it out of winnings, lock, stock and barrel.

Charlie sober might have shied off but Charlie drunk was quite willing to go into business. They decided on a big opening with the first round of drinks upon the house, but their friends, and friends's friends, and friends' friends' friends came from miles around and drank the place dry before midnight. When they counted up the cash they found they had taken in about twelve dollars, all the rest had been on the house. There was nothing to salvage so they shook hands on it and nailed up the door and never went back. This was Charlie's only business venture.

I have heard other versions of this story but they all ended up the same way.

That summer the Russells had an exhibition at the Calgary Rodeo and when they closed the house to go to Canada, Bill Krieghoff and I went up to Lake McDonald to open camp. With just the two of us we found it extremely lonely. As always after nine months' absence, needles and twigs and so forth—the winter's windfall—had drifted over everything; all outlines were blurred. You could see that it would need only a few years' emptiness for the cabin itself to bog down and become again part of the woods.

"Now if we just had a couple of girls!" said Bill who had a weakness for ladies.

I would have wasted the morning exploring the trails but Bill was more conscientious, so we turned to and put in a hard days' work, dug out the spring of ice water—it always filled up with cedar fronds and a queer black oozy muck as rich as velvet—got up on top of the cabin and cleaned the needles out from between the shakes (if you don't, the roof will leak) and swept out the living room and got lunch and supper.

Somebody had given Aunt Nancy a gilded cow-bell with a red ribbon which she used as a dinner bell—you could hear it a long way through the woods, much further than a voice —and when we finished the roof and began to clean the living room, I hung the bell outside the back door in the open dog-run between the cabin and the kitchen. In Missouri the dog-run is a roofed-over porch between two cabins.

That night when we were turning in—Bill already in bed and I standing by the table about to blow out the lamp —the bell gave a sudden and startling clang. Just one—it didn't keep on jingling as a cow-bell does after you give it a shake. It rang that once, then stopped entirely, exactly as it would if you rang it and then put your hand on it to kill the vibration. (I had a very vivid picture of a grizzly standing up on his hindlegs, trying to look in over the top of the door, accidentally striking the bell and then immediately putting his paw on it to stop it. In fact, I have that picture yet, it startled me so, that sudden clang in the silence of the forest.)

Bill, equally startled, said: "Who did that?"

Me, whispering: "I guess a trade-rat must have jumped against it."

"I haven't heard any rats," said Bill (they're noisy pests —you can hear their every move up on the roof) "and anyhow no rat would put his paw on the bell to silence it. His paws aren't big enough." So Bill had the same mental picture —a bear or something tall enough to reach the bell and intelligent enough to muffle it.

"Maybe it's some joker trying to scare us." We were a mile from the nearest camp and I never knew any joker to go prowling around in the pine woods at night where you can't walk a yard without stumbling over a root or a down tree.

By then Bill was out of bed and shouted in a big voice as if he were seven feet tall, "Who is it?"

No answer, not a sound; the whole forest held its breath. So did we.

"Well, we better find out!" said Bill: so he took the poker and the lantern—the double-bitted ax was outside, stuck in the wood block—and I got the .22 automatic we used on rats; and we opened the door, very cautiously, and looked out and saw nothing except the leaping shadows and the empty dog-run; and finally we went out and poked around—getting braver every minute—but never discovered who or what rang the bell, rang it and then silenced it so suggestively.

"It's silly," said Bill, "but just the same I'm glad I'm not here alone."

179

So was I—fear shared is fear cut in half but fear alone is fear doubled.

Such fears vanished before the morning sun and I didn't hear a cow-bell again till I went to get the mail. There was an old beaver meadow back in the woods which Apgar used as a pasture, and as I went by on the road I heard the bell clanging fast, and here, at a clumsy gallop, came a milk cow with bag swinging, and face down across her back and kicking her ribs was a small boy in knee britches.

He knew I came from the Charlie Russell camp and slid down and let the cow walk and informed me that his family were staying in one of Apgar's cabins and especially that his cousin, the delectable Polly—which isn't her name—was staying with them. I had seen Polly in Great Falls and admired her from a distance—she couldn't see me, being too surrounded by boys—but here at the Lake where there was no competition she could and did behold me. Behold and waylay. Every morning when I went to get the mail Polly was there, giggling. Being Charlie's nephew had something to do with this and also the aforesaid lack of competition. There seemed to be no other young men around. I was, as always, not very enterprising: I never went near her in the afternoon and never thought of inviting her to camp.

This continued after the Russells came down from Canada where they met the Duke and Duchess of Connaught. Connaught, mind you, an Irish title, and he was so Teutonic and spoke such thick and gutteral English that Charlie could hardly understand him, while his wife was just plain *hausfrau*. Very plain. Charlie also met the famous Princess Pat and either then or later her royal cousin the Prince of Wales—now Duke of Windsor—and sold him a painting of the Northwest Mounted.

"You know," said Charlie, summing it up, "Bill Rance with his yellow mustache—especially when he's had a couple of drinks—looks more like a duke in five minutes than these English royalties would in twenty years. His Grace of Connaught ought to be selling sausages—God gave him just the figger to fill an apron."

But Nancy was, as always, much more American: she thought Princess Pat really lovely, while as for Wales—well, as we would say nowadays, he was just out of this world. Thus Nancy, her very soul kowtowing.

She, of course, was the one who sold the picture. Swooning with admiration for your victims is a sure way to sell pictures.

But let's get back to Polly. As I did every morning.

Except when we were out in the canoe her family were always around, grinning and goggling; and they shrieked with laughter when Polly announced that she had made a "poem" about me, which she recited, sparkling:

"Green leaves Russell in the morning."

(Rustle and Russell, get the subtlety of it?)

That's all there was—just that one line. In those days I had a notion that girls were not very bright but this seemed a singularly pointless joke even for a girl.

But it had point all right, my trouble being that I didn't know the context. For there *was* a Green, a tall, skinny, amorous and irascible Mr. Green who drove the afternoon stage. Mornings he clerked in the store at Belton; it was only after noon that he saw Polly; and I, fetching the mail, saw her only ante-meridian. Now Green knew about me but I didn't know about Green.

Then came the noon when we met. Low noon for me. It was just my luck to have Charlie and Bill row over with me that day. The stage was in; everybody saw us coming in the rowboat. And there on the beach, on the jingling, jangling pebbles, Green was waiting. He asked what I meant by

181

poaching on his preserves or words to that effect. Though taken by surprise I made a witty answer. The rest of the plot is too painful—why resurrect a lot of bloody knuckles and black eyes? The knuckles were mostly his'n, the eyes mine. I never met anyone so overstocked with knuckles.

Charlie's brutal side came out: he seemed to think it funny. He displayed no trace of tribal solidarity; it never even occurred to him to avenge me.

Bill, of course, was in raptures.

The next day was even worse. Somebody—I don't remember who—had a couple of horses at Apgar's and offered to let Bill and Charlie ride them up the old Oil Road to a big beaver meadow back in the hills. As it fell out, Charlie and Nancy had to go to the head of the Lake to see a prospective picture-buyer, so I rode with Bill instead. Polly, her kid cousin and several others accompanied us when we went to get the horses. We discovered that they were bridled but not saddled—the saddles were at the Post Office.

I had never ridden bareback and when I laid my hand on the horse's withers, that convenient hump at the top of the shoulder, and vaulted into place astride his back, I, so to say, over-vaulted. I couldn't stop there. His back was slick, there were no handles or anything to catch hold of, and I slid right off the other side and fell flat on my stomach. I was slim then and had practically no stomach but I contrived somehow to light on it and it knocked the wind out of me.

Alarmed by my thunderous fall, Polly and the others all asked, "Are you hurt? Are you hurt?"

Of course, I was hurt but I couldn't say so, couldn't say anything but Awk!—run around in a circle, hold on to my stomach and say, "Awk! Awk!"

Bill, as unsympathetic as he had been at the massacre on the beach, called me the Great Auk. The Auk—if you don't happen to know—is an arctic bird; he traverses the frozen wastes of the pole on tireless wing and no matter what wonders he may see—white rainbows, triple suns, the flaming splendors of the aurora borealis—all he says is "Auk!"

Which perhaps offended Providence and explains his now being extinct.

But it was Polly who hurt me most. As soon as she saw I wasn't actually broken in two, she went back to Apgar's and told everybody, "*He* got on the horse: the horse started to walk, *he* fell off."

Surely those were horses of humiliation. I led them—no more vaulting—to the Post Office and saddled up and we mounted, Bill still being funny about the Great Auk. I was cautious, he was not; the horses had not been exercised for a week. At the first touch of the spur Bill's charger bolted and started at a dead run not across the bridge and up to the beaver meadow but straight down the road to Belton. It was a snaffle, not a spade-bit, and Bill had no more control over his mount than if he were riding an avalanche. He "pulled leather," got a death grip on the saddle horn, and even so it was all he could do to stay on.

I followed at a gallop—I knew enough to keep my horse's head up and not let him run—but didn't overtake him till we got to the very bottom of Belton Hill. By that time I was scared—afraid his horse would miss the sharp turn at the bridge and hurl over the bank into the Flathead River.

However, the horse stopped of its own accord and we turned back toward Apgar's. Bill complained that his BVDs had rolled up his leg and chafed him but he didn't dare get down and investigate—he was afraid the horse wouldn't let him mount again—so we rode all the way to the Beaver Meadow, a lonely, haunted-looking place, knee-deep in rustling yellow grass and walled all around the edge with solemn pine trees. Over their tops, as if craning up on tiptoe to stare at us, we saw the snow mountains.

It was noon by then and we dismounted and drank at the creek and ate our sandwiches and let the horses graze; but when we came to mount again Bill let out a yell as soon as he touched the saddle. This time he did investigate and discovered that five inches of hide had been removed from the inner side of his thighs; the BVDs, rolled up in a ridge, had rasped him like a file. He couldn't ride; he walked all the way back to camp; I led his horse, and it was nearly a week before he healed.

By way of consoling him, Charlie wrote on the screen which served as the camp register:

> Hark to the saga of Duck-leg Bill
> Who ran his horse down Belton Hill:
> He kept his seat to all's surprise
> Tho skinned from his knees plumb up to his thighs.

At Apgar's they pointed us out to tourists as the Twin Horsemen of Bull's Head Lodge. "The funny looking one fell off when his horse started to walk. The other stayed on but he rode himself raw behind."

21

Anecdotes Of Lake McDonald

Charlie's summer camp was built in a clearing a hundred yards up the hill and in front the ground sloped steeply down to the lake, a slope carpeted, every inch of it, not with grass but with glossy and slippery pine needles the color of bronze. Rising like columns from that shining floor, and as straight as if drawn with a ruler, the trees stood up in their ranks all around the clearing. There was no underbrush—the slope looked as if it had been swept that morning.

In front of the main cabin was a porch of hewed logs so wide it was really a terrace. There, on warm days, Charlie worked at his easel. A monumental stair, also of hewed logs, led up to the porch. There was nothing flimsy or rickety, no Southern shanty look to cabin or porch or stair; all were solid and massive as stonework. And they were not bleached or whitewashed like a Missouri cabin—these logs were a dark cedar red. The roof, of course, was cedar and shone in the sun.

The trees rising tier on tier, a hundred feet above the top of the chimney, concentrated the sunlight and funneled it down; on a bright day the whole clearing glowed. Approaching through the timber you would see the glowing open, all gold and amber, and up the slope and watching you—and mysterious looking—the cabin, dark and secretive under its eaves. The brighter the day the darker the eyes, which is to say the windows, of a log cabin. It may be as bare as a barn inside; it always seems to hide secrets.

Charlie's cabin had secrets too, but I didn't know them.

Behind the main cabin, at right angles to it, and joined to it by a "dog-run," was the kitchen cabin, and behind that a long shed, just roof and uprights, for firewood.

Apgar built the cabins and the porch, but Charlie supplied the two figures that guarded the stair. They were eighteen inches high, an Indian and a Gnome, not carved but pieced together out of twisted roots and odd-shaped twigs and branches. The Gnome had hair of green moss, the Indian of black. The pine woods are full of greenish-gray moss but the black is hard to find. On our walks through the timber Charlie was always on the lookout for black moss and for queer and suggestive bits of roots and branches. Several times every summer the trade-rats stole the black moss from the Indian; they wouldn't touch the green.

Both these figures were lean and angular, neither had a white beard, neither wore a red coat or boots, and yet visitors almost invariably exclaimed, "Oh look, Santa Claus!"

Apparently Santa Claus is America's only mythology.

Beside the guardians of the stair, Charlie made smaller figures down by the spring, both Indian and white, a lodge or teepee, and a miniature log cabin. But these, not being nailed down, had to be taken in whenever we left camp because tourists stole them. However, there weren't many tourists; there were no cabins beyond ours on that side of the Lake and weeks would go by without anyone coming near us.

And without people there is peace, especially in the pine forests of the Rockies, so much more silent than the Missouri woods. That is the first impression the mountains make on you—Here Is Peace.

Too peaceful for Charlie who was beginning to get middle-aged and restless. After a few days in camp with only the family around he wanted to "see people." Except right at summer's end they always had three or four guests; one summer they had eighteen at one time. Which was like running a hotel; it was also very expensive. Every ounce of food had to be brought in from Kalispell and Columbia Falls, and in the mountains people who at home live on salad and crullers eat like lumberjacks three times a day.

That summer there were real lumberjacks in the forest. Of course, they couldn't fell trees in the Forest Reserve but Apgar had sold part of his timber and if you went to the foot of the Lake you could hear the axes all day, and the saw, and the cry of warning, and the unmistakable sound of the falling tree, which hurt Charlie so that he wouldn't go there. But the rest of us did, and watched them at work, and crossed over the crest to the steep hill above the Flathead River and the deep groove in the slope where they snaked the logs down to the water. They didn't need to build a flume.

The groove was black and polished like the slot worn by Fafnir between the Rhinegold and the Rhine down which at dawn each day he went to drink. Fafnir, you know, had been a man until the gold he hoarded turned him into a snake, the Long-Worm of the swamp.

> And lo, amid the ruin,
>   a monstrous serpent rolled:
> And I knew that that worm was Fafnir,
>   the wallower on the gold.

The American Fafnir, Big Business, was now wallowing —and making a ruin—of the woods right at the edge of our National Park, and Charlie was the only one in camp with sense enough to resent it. The rest of us, being good Americans, just watched the worm at work, awestruck by his glittering efficiency.

187

For ceremonial and magical reasons the plains Indian sometimes carried a Coup-Stick, decorated with feathers and as long as a lance but usually curved at the top like a shepherd's crook. Charlie didn't carry a Coup-Stick but he carved several canes for use on the trail. You need a cane in the morning because the big gray spiders of the country spin their webs, head-high, right across the trail and the best way to keep from getting a face-full is to hold a cane in front of you as you go along.

What monkey sees, monkey does. I also tried my hand at canes and carved a gaudy toucan, red, green, yellow and black, with a beak so big you could hook it over your arm. Charlie's own cane was headed with an Owl. The Gray Owl was the medicine man of the Little People, dwarfish creatures the Indians saw at dusk. They stood knee-high to a man, just about the size of the two guardians of Charlie's stair, and dressed like full-sized Indians but it wasn't safe to see them because they were wizards and didn't like to be spied on. In both name and in nature they corresponded very closely to the Little People of the Irish peasants. In *Hiawatha* it was these Little People who lay in wait for Kwasind the Strong Man and caught him asleep in his canoe and killed him with pine cones. I remember writing a "theme" on that in school.

Charlie was always experimenting. The forest is full of fungi of different kinds, and one kind which forms in a sort of shelf at the foot of trees is black and ugly underneath but on top a beautiful creamy white or a soft pearl-gray or fawn-color, and you can write or draw on it with a pin. Charlie drew little figures, deer and so forth, but you never could tell what that particular piece of fungus would do—sometimes the whole top turned black and leathery, sometimes the picture just faded away like ghost-writing, but sometimes it stayed gray or fawn-color with the drawing etched on it in a deep rich brown. Often, in a mysterious fashion, just part of the picture would fade.

Here's an improbable happening:

Back of the cabins and at the up-edge of the clearing was a hole and in it a pile of tin cans. One morning when Krieghoff and I were alone he saw a weasel run into the pile. He called me and I got the .22 automatic and we beat on the pile and poked around in it with a stick but the weasel sat tight and said nothing. Finally, on the off chance that the reverberation would scare him out, I shoved the muzzle into an opening between the cans and fired. A .22 doesn't reverberate very convincingly, not even in a pile of tin cans, and the weasel still lay low.

An hour later Bill went that way again, and there, six feet from the pile and stretched out flat, his nose yearning toward the woods, was a dead weasel with a bullet hole in his neck.

I don't expect you to believe this. I hardly believe it myself and yet it happened.

When Charlie came back from the head of the Lake he sat down on his heels and skinned the weasel and stretched it on a little frame to dry—a bent twig made the frame and the bend, trying to straighten itself, kept the skin stretched taut—and he took it back to Great Falls, where it hung for years in his studio. He also at various times skinned and dried several trade-rat pelts. They have a nice gray fur, white underneath, but as soon as you dry it the hair comes out in patches and makes it look mangy and motheaten.

It always surprised and frequently offended practical people to see Charlie devote just as much effort and care and skill to this sort of thing as to his most important picture. Whatever he did it was a pleasure to watch him, he was so deft with his hands; with slightly different brain convolutions he would have made a great surgeon. As an eastern highbrow remarked, to see Charlie throw a one-man diamond hitch was an esthetic experience. I looked the word up in Nancy's high school dictionary and thenceforth spoke with authority on the subject. Which Charlie endured quite patiently but Nancy sometimes rebelled and remarked that after all Charlie was the artist, not me.

But to get back to the weasel. The reason Bill and I were so anxious to kill him was that Nancy had brought up to camp a crate full of chickens. They were not fenced in, they never left the clearing, I never saw one venture into the woods; but they did so well in the open, scratching up bugs and things, and their combs were so red—which, according to Charlie, is a sign of health and happiness—and kept up such a contented clucking all day that it was a pleasure to hear them. There wasn't a rooster within a hundred miles but the hens didn't seem to care.

"What?" asked Charlie, straightening up from the two-man saw to contemplate the chickens—we were always straightening up from the two-man saw, willing to contemplate anything except the saw—"what does a rooster win by his fine feathers and all his strutting and bragging? The hens never look at him. The only time they know he's around is when he gives them the works—and that lasts less than a minute."

Whereupon Bill, who was quite a rooster himself and wore his hair *en brosse* like yellow feathers and strutted and stuck out his chest, told an early modern joke about a hen crossing the highway and being run over by a Ford. When it had gone on she got up and shook her feathers and said, "My goodness, what a rough rooster!"

"She was as flattered," quoth Bill, "as a middle-aged woman who gets her tail slapped by a drunk."

Now these hens of Charlie's were strictly an urban product, born and bred in the city—Great Falls calls itself a city—since issuing from the egg they had never seen a chicken hawk or an eagle or any bird of prey. Yet when at noon a big fish-hawk flew over the clearing—he didn't scream or circle or descend, just swooped overhead, high up, on his wide wings—the hens were so terrified that they hid all the rest of the day. How did they know? At sundown Charlie and I, rounding them up, found two wedged in behind a big trunk in the dog-run.

Did you ever hear the coffin-bird back in the woods making his coffin—you never see him—and the hollow sound as he drops the lid and hops around on it to make sure it is soul-tight?

Even the woodpecker, the wise little peckerwood, of no importance whatever in the bird-full woodlands of Missouri, becomes quite an impressive person in the empty and silent pine forest of the Rockies. He's bigger and black with just one streak of red feathers on his crest. You go alone along the trail and off to the right—and so close that you feel sure you can see him by stooping under the branches— you hear a lumberjack at work, chop! chop! chop! It sounds exactly like an axe. Suddenly it stops—as if he heard you coming—a black bird flies across the trail, and in a minute you hear the axe again, off to the left.

Back in the woods, away from the lake, there was another woodcutter, in human form, whom I never heard but saw several times from a distance.

If you went up the old abandoned trail back of the cabin, up over the hill, you came to the old abandoned "oil road," and if you went up the road a couple of miles, past one of my landmarks, a broken, split-open tree which the ants or termites or something had tunneled into a delicate brown lacework of arcades and galleries and balconies, you

191

came at last to a side trail not made by man—the woods are full of them—a long natural alley-way leading off into the timber, and if it was the right hour of the evening, and if the light was just so, there, at the far end of that alley-way, you saw—and it startled you, having thought yourself entirely alone—a woodsman standing there quite still with one hand on his axe. He made no sound, he didn't do anything, just stood there. It was too far to see his face but his pose showed he was watching you. He looked intensely real. And very tall.

I knew it was illusion, an effect of the light through the branches; I knew that if I went down that alley-way he would vanish; but I was a cowardly pup, I never went there, just watched him from the road as he watched me.

I went back several evenings and saw him. He always gave the effect of having stopped whatever he was up to just when he heard me coming.

I told Charlie but it was a long walk and nobody in camp would go that far to look at an illusion, which, were there two of us, might not be there.

Here is the only white man's ghost story I ever heard Charlie tell. He told it in an appropriate setting. It was after supper, the sun had gone but there was still light in the sky, we had just returned from a packtrip up over Gunsight Pass and there must have been a dozen of us sitting around a fire on the beach, before us the lake, as still and as smooth as a mirror, and at our backs the pine forest as black as ink. I went to get more firewood and missed the first part of the story and so didn't learn until later where Charlie got it. I supposed he heard it from one of the hunters he met when he was with Jake Hoover.

The story concerned two trappers who followed a branch of the river up a likely looking valley and saw plenty of old beaver signs. This was in early days when the mountains were still unexplored, when there wasn't a clearing anywhere except those made by the beavers.

The farther they went up the valley the thicker the timber got—too thick for packs—so when they came to an old beaver meadow with good grass they unsaddled and turned loose the horses and made camp. There were still a couple hours of daylight so they went afoot up along the river to where it forked, and they agreed that next morning Bill would go up the north fork and Jim up the south and string their traps—a very lonely business.

When they got back to the meadow, the horses weren't grazing but hiding in the edge of the timber and a bear or something had messed up their camp, broken down the windbreak they made and knocked things around. Jim began to rebuild the windbreak but Bill said, "You notice anything funny about those tracks?"

Jim looked: "Well, they're very big. It's a grizzly—not a black bear."

"Notice anything else?"

"No, what do you mean?"

"That bear's walking on his hind feet."

Sure enough, they couldn't find any place where he had got down on all fours.

Of course, a bear *does* rare up on his hind legs to look around or to claw a tree, and sometimes he walks a few paces that way but never very far.

That night they were woke up by something big smashing around in the timber and moaning and carrying on, and it made Bill so uneasy—especially the moaning, which was terrible—that he built up a bright fire and lay awake with his rifle until almost daybreak, but Jim went back to sleep.

Next morning early they set out to string their traps, and Bill hadn't been alone an hour before he began to get scary. There didn't seem to be any game at all, not even pine squirrels or chipmunks; no birds—nothing—and yet he got the notion he was being followed. He backtracked a couple of times but didn't see anything.

As soon as he had set his traps he hurried home to the meadow and was surprised to see smoke going up and his partner already starting to get supper. Jim seemed glad to see him, and they ate and smoked and started to roll out the blankets, and then Jim surprised him again by saying, "I got plenty wood—let's keep the fire going and take turns to watch."

They did—and nothing happened. Along in the night they thought they heard that moaning up the valley, but it was far off. Later, on towards morning, in Bill's watch, he heard it coming back again, but it stopped at the edge of the timber. Evidently the bear was afraid of the fire.

Although they hadn't really seen anything—except those tracks—Bill was more uneasy than ever, but ashamed to say so; and he was glad when Jim spoke up at breakfast and said, "I don't like this place—let's get out of here," and they agreed to pick up their traps and pull out that afternoon as soon as they could and get outside the valley before sundown. They didn't say so but they had a strong notion, both of them, that it wouldn't do to stay another night.

Bill collected his traps on a high lope and hurried back to the meadow, expecting to be first; but when he got to the edge of the trees he saw smoke going up and one horse already packed, and there was Jim sitting by the fire and taking it easy, leaning back against an old down tree.

"Thank God!" said Bill, who didn't usually do much praying, and he looked at the sun and thought, "We got lots of time," and it seemed kind of foolish to haul tail just because they saw a few bear tracks. And they were both old mountain men who had been trapping for years.

He called, but Jim didn't answer or even look around, and Bill went toward him, and all of a sudden it struck him that Jim was sitting with his head bent back in a queer way as if he was looking straight up. And there wasn't anything to look at but the sky—no eagles, no fish-hawks, nothing.

Before he got to the fire, Bill knew his partner was dead—his neck was broken. Tracks back of the log showed what happened. The bear—or whatever it was—still walking on its hindlegs and taking long strides like a man—had crept upon Jim from behind and grabbed his head with its forepaws and bent it back and snapped his neck.

Bill didn't stop for any funeral. He dropped his traps and got out of there right away.

This story, told by the campfire, so impressed me—of course, Charlie didn't tell it quite this baldly and briefly—that next morning I urged him to write it and get it printed.

"No," said Charlie, "other things being equal I'd rather not go to jail."

"What's jail got to do with it?"

"Well, in the first place, it's not my story. In the second place, it's already been printed and read all over the world. And in the third place if I tried to steal it, Teddy Roosevelt wouldn't just break my neck—he'd tear my head off."

When we went back to town I verified and found it in Roosevelt's book, and noted especially his remark that he suspected it was really a piece of European folklore, the old trapper who told it, though born in this country, being of German stock.

It doesn't sound western. The Indians, of course, told ghost stories—the plains tribes were always afraid of the timber—and they had plenty of were-animals, bear-men, wolf-men, bird-men and so forth; but we have wiped out the Indians' culture, the white man despises this sort of foolishness and in all Montana there isn't even a second- or third-rate ghost.

If you want to compare Charlie's version—he had forgotten some details and put in others of his own—you will find the original on page 441 of Roosevelt's *The Wilderness Hunter*.

There was another bit of folklore current out West which I heard when I first went to Montana—the joke about the tenderfoot who asked for a job at a sheep ranch. They said No, but he was so insistent that they finally told him to separate the lambs from the sheep and drive them into the corral. He was gone for hours and when at last he came in, long after supper, he said he had the most trouble with the little one with long ears.

They didn't know what he meant by a lamb with long ears, so they went out to see and found he had run down a jack rabbit. And if you ever saw a jack take off across the prairie you know that calls for speed.

This is a very ancient story not only in Europe but in Asia and told in particular of Perceval the Grail Hero, the innocent fool, who was so ignorant, and so agile, that when they sent him out to catch the goats he also caught a doe; and he described her as the big one who had lost her horns through running wild in the wood. They too didn't know what he meant by a goat without horns, and they too went out to see.

When we broke camp, Bill Krieghoff returned with us to Great Falls, stayed there for months, painted an excellent portrait of old Mr. Trigg, a full length one, not so good, of Nancy, and others of Charlie, Albertine Raban, and Ben MacNair's daughter—this last, I think, his first professional, i.e., ordered-and-paid-for, portrait. When he finally went back to New York he found he had been away from home too long—Julie had grown used to doing without him, and the next we knew they were divorced.

Bill married again, was devoted, so we heard, to his new wife, and set himself up in earnest as a portrait painter. He was successful and began to make a name for himself; but his wife died, and then Bill died, still comparatively young.

A generation later, after World War II, I went through the card index in the art room at the New York Library. No mention of either Krieghoff or Philip Goodwin—two good artists, both New Yorkers, and nothing to show they ever existed.

❦ 22 ❧

The Give-Away Dance

Charlie had written and illustrated several short stories and got good pay for them and the editors asked for more, but it was like pulling teeth to get him to write. Drawing, he said, was natural like breathing; but writing was hard work like carving a stone. And he didn't think much of his carving.

"*You* write it," he said when I kept urging him, and he told a story to me in detail but I was never able to write it. If I tried to put it in his words, it sounded stiff and un-natural; if I put it in mine there was no story.

Here, as nearly as I can recall, is how it went:

The Ky-yuse Indians often came over the mountains to trade for horses with the prairie tribes and sometimes they saw a girl they liked and traded women. Which is how Buffalo Horn, a Crow warrior, got him a Ky-yuse wife named Red Belt. She was a big, tall, fine-looking girl and the Crow women eyed her over and didn't like her; they looked at her sideways and thought her too proud for a stranger.

Buffalo Horn didn't care what the women thought: she was good lovin' and he kept her several years, but they had no babies and in the end he got tired of her. He showed it and her pride came out and she began quarreling with him and spoke words that bit into his heart and made him hate her. Which is easy to do for people of different tribes.

This time he didn't show it and she was too proud and too sure of herself to guess what he intended.

198

The Give-Away Dance

Some say the Indians were socialists. They were not, but they didn't have the strong property sense of the white man. The Indian owned the weapons he made and the horses he stole or captured in war, but the whole tribe hunted the buffalo in common—followed the herd like a pack of wolves —and everybody gorged or starved at the same time. There was no extreme wealth or abject poverty, and especially there was nothing to compare with the vast difference in outlook and interest which separates the modern workers from the rich man. (Of course, Charlie didn't go into all these details.) Among the prairie tribes everybody worked a little, and everybody loafed a lot. Hence the ancient joke, "the Indians do nothing except hunt, fish and frig, and in winter there is no hunting or fishing—"

Not only did the Indian lack property sense; if he accidentally got a lot of possessions he was apt some day when he was feeling good to call the camp to a feast, a Give-Away Dance.

That's what Buffalo Horn did. He called the whole tribe to a feast and when they had eaten he stood up and made his talk and gave away all his possessions till he had nothing left except his lodge, his horses, his gun and his wife.

"Stand up," said he to Red Belt, and he took her by the upper arm and turned her around, this way, that way, in the firelight, and showed her to the people, saying, "Here is a woman from over the mountains, a big, tall, healthy girl; but I wouldn't give her to a friend—I wouldn't want to hurt him. I wouldn't give her even to an enemy; I'm not going to give her to anybody—I'm going to *throw* her away! Anybody who wants her can have her." And he gripped her arm and swung her with all his strength and sent her spinning clear across the circle.

You can imagine how the women laughed.

Red Belt had not known what he intended but she knew better than to stay there by the fire. She ran right through the people down to the creek and hid in the brush till dark. She was ashamed and her heart was on the ground; but also she was full of hate and the longer she crouched there among the willows the harder her hate got. She wanted to kill Buffalo Horn who threw her away and do it in such a fashion that it would shame the whole tribe, yes, the whole Crow Nation. But it wouldn't shame them if they caught her doing it, caught her and killed her.

At first she didn't know what to do.

The plains Indians had no discipline and almost no organization: except in war time they kept no watch—they trusted that to the dogs.

But the dogs knew Red Belt's smell; they recognized her farther than they could see her and they didn't even snarl when just before moonrise she crept into the lodge. She could hear Buffalo Horn breathing and knew right where he lay but it took her a long time to crawl up to him and roll down the blanket and count his ribs and find the place to put the knife point—warming it first in her armpit so that the cold of the white man's steel wouldn't wake him—and hold it steady, just barely touching, and raise her other hand with clenched fist and hit the handle with all her strength. She hit it, and the knife went in like *that*—right into his heart.

He jerked all over and she grabbed the blanket and held it to his mouth but he didn't even groan.

She got down the white man's gun where it hung in its sheath from the lodge poles, and flint and steel, and hatchet, and ball and powder, and a skin of dried meat; and then she put a final shame on the dead man. She slipped off her breech-clout from between her legs and laid it flat across Buffalo Horn's face ("Of course," said Charlie, "you couldn't put *that* in") and she laughed at him in the dark, being careful not to laugh aloud; and she raised the door-flap and crept out of the lodge, and out of the camp, and crossed the creek, and caught the best horse—an Apaloos—and by the time she got into the timber up the valley, one of the dogs had smelled the blood and put back its head and howled. He kept on howling till the others came over and sniffed around the lodge, and they too put up their heads and howled. They made the whole hollow ring.

(Here Charlie put back *his* head and howled; but you can't do that in print.)

Haven't thought of it for years, but now, writing it, I can see Charlie standing in the near-dusk of the evening cabin—*would* have been dusk except for the big skylight overhead—with paint on his palette thumb and in his other hand a cigaret and he gesticulating as he always did whenever he told a story. He was as intent as if, almost, he identified himself with Red Belt on her Apaloos horse up in the fringe of the timber looking down at the camp which had been her home and listening to the dogs howling. He made her seem not a bit less tragic than Argive Klytemnestra.

"Now don't overwrite it," said Charlie, describing her flight to the mountains and up over them with the Crows hot on her heels, "and don't put in any poetry! Don't quote Homer or Omer or Gomer." (For Charlie knew that both Homer and Omar were poets but wasn't sure which was which.) "Just tell it short and plain like an Indian would."

But we never profit by advice; despite his warning, Klytemnestra got in.

I couldn't write the stories Charlie told me, but he could and did put in pictures what I told him. I have a large unfinished watercolor which is unique—the only Aztec picture Charlie ever painted. It illustrates a story I told him and it doesn't look like Charlie's work at all; the change of subject has somehow changed his style.

Unless you have tried it, you cannot imagine what a seductive pleasure it is to have in the house an important but uneducated artist to whom you can impart all sorts of miscellaneous information. And Charlie was wonderfully patient; though he seldom believed what I told him he never refused to let me tell it.

It was my habit to search with the eye of an eagle—or of a buzzard—for cultural items with which to enlighten his ignorance, and somewhere, probably at the public library, I came across one of the choicest gems in the treasury of modern art: how the Dutch artist Vincent Van Gogh went with his tough boy friend (Gauguin) to a bawdy house where one of the girls, unable to admire anything else about him, professed to admire his ears; she said they were "jolie." Poor Van, unused to female admiration, was so overwhelmed that he went home and cut off the ear and sent it to her in a box.

"I bet that's a damn lie," said Charlie. "Some other artist invented it, somebody who was jealous of his painting."

Charlie himself was the least jealous of men, and it was funny—or rather it was revealing—how many visitors thought to win his favor by attacking other artists. I remember a writer of two-gun westerns who cut loose with a diatribe against Frederick Remington, then, saying that he was a newspaper man, not an artist; that he could draw only one kind of horse and one kind of man; that the only way to tell a Remington cowboy from a Remington Indian was that the cowboy wore a flop hat and a big yellow mustache; that Remington himself got so grossly fat that he couldn't ride horseback but had to be hauled around in a cart like a prize pig; and, finally, that he died of overeating.

The Give-Away Dance

"You suppose it's true?" I asked when the writer had gone.

"Well, he did get fat," said Charlie, "and he died comparatively young, but that, as Bill Krieghoff would say, is not a 'valid' criticism of his art." When Charlie used a word like "valid" or other bits of critical jargon, he always put it in quotation marks to show it wasn't his. He couldn't help picking up some of the talk he heard in New York studios but he always regarded it as artificial imported stuff, appropriate, perhaps, to Europe but not to us.

"I'll bet," said Charlie, "that years from now when some critic compares our pictures," (for as the result of hearing it so often he had accepted the idea, at first unthought of, that his work was historically important) "what he'll notice is that Russell and Remington saw the same country but not the same colors, and *that's* all a difference of light."

As he got older, Charlie laid less and less stress on drawing and composition and more and more on light. I suppose he got this at second or third or fourth hand from the French Impressionists who were, they say, the first to realize the part played by light and how it breaks up color. Got it, of course, not by reading or study but from the people he met in New York.

Not that Charlie was an admirer of French art. Years later when my sister was married and had a family and a home of her own, Charlie and Nancy visited her in Milwaukee and she took them to the Art Museum. The director showed them around and pointed out a Corot. Charlie looked at it and said, "I wouldn't hang that in my chicken house."

Nancy started to smooth this over but their guide admitted it was not a very good Corot. In plain words it was a "name picture," bought not because it was worth keeping but because Corot signed it. Most museums are full of name pictures.

203

✍ 23 ❧

Charlie And Nancy As Partners

Probably it's a good thing Charlie lived so far from the
city and went there only once a year—often every other year
—and had long months between to chew over what he saw
and heard. Chew it over and reject a lot of it. Of course, in
those days New York was only an outpost of Europe. American artists of the traditional kind still wanted to go to Paris
or Rome or London or even Berlin.

In one way Charlie was lucky. Although he lived long
enough to see the end of the old West, he died before the
famous "American Dream" so unaccountably developed into
something with all the earmarks of delirium tremens. This
doesn't mean that Europe gave us D.T.s. We Americans did
it ourselves; some Mammon-poison in us, a hardening of the
arteries of the soul, a spiritual elephantiasis.

Yes, Charlie was lucky—luckier, for instance, than Joe
DeYong who was born a long generation late. We first
heard of Joe when he was about fourteen and sent Charlie
a comical little wax horse and rider. Charlie wrote back a
very nice letter but he didn't think the little figure showed
any particular aptitude. There may have been other letters
which I have forgotten but when, two or three years later,
Joe appeared in the flesh, he had by dint of plain hard work
and pertinacity become an unmistakable artist.

Both Charlie and Nancy fell for him at the first meeting.
So did the Triggs.

Joe was black-haired and of what he called "fox-terrier build," small, slim, alert, always up on his toes. Born in Missouri—St. Louis County—but bred in the west, he had worked, quite young, as a rider in the movies. On location, shooting some western picture, they were caught in a sudden snow storm—and they in their shirts and all sweated up with hard riding—and kept out in the wet snow for hours by a stubborn director, with the result that many of them got sick and Joe caught a chill which developed into pneumonia.

Out of evil good and so forth—it was during his long convalescence that he began to work seriously as an artist. Without that spell of sickness he might have gone on as a movie extra, devoloping logically into an actor and perhaps, with good luck, a star. But things didn't work out that way.

Staying with the Russells a week or ten days at a time and working out in the studio he soon learned the Indian Sign Talk.

Joe was a reader and already knew, theoretically, more about modern trends than Charlie, but as a western product his ideas of art were quite different from those expressed by Krieghoff and Marchand and Young-Hunter and the other painters I had heard hold forth. His interests were entirely western and the danger was that admiring Charlie so intensely he would become just a lesser C.M.R. But, as time showed, he was strong enough to keep his individuality.

That summer, 1915—Charlie was fifty-one—Joe went up with us to Lake McDonald, and inspired by The-Thing-in-the-Forest, the suggestion so much stronger than on the prairie of presences other than human, he began almost at once to write a fantasy story—not meant for print—of the creatures he saw or imagined in the shadows. Charlie got interested and joined in with suggestions of his own—good perhaps but different—and then came something which impressed me greatly. Joe—and it took no particular insight to see how he hated to do it—spunked up and did what I could never have done, came out and said, flat and plain, what was in his heart. Namely, that Charlie's imaginings clashed with his and that he, Joe, must write the story his own way.

This called for real moral courage.

Charlie took it well—he would—and was not offended, and they got along together as nicely as before, but Joe wrote his own stories.

Now Joe worshiped Charlie's tracks and I concluded that if he could do this he was in no danger of being diluted and subverted, as many an apprentice is by the overwhelming presence of the master.

When I met Joe again, many years later, he was on intimate terms with Will Rogers—who called him Jodee—Bill Hart and other notables, and was again working for the movies (Paramount), not as an actor but as an artist and an authority on Indian dress and Indian ways.

I still have a rhyme, a western Rubaiyat, he wrote as a kid:

> A fire,
> A can,
> An Irish stew:
> The moon,
> The stars,
> And me and you.

and a line drawing of two tramps cooking supper in the lee of a railroad embankment.

Charlie and Nancy would both have liked to adopt Joe but he was too big and had besides a couple of practicing parents of his own who seemed to be quite fond of him.

When I first went to Montana they had wanted to adopt Skookum, as Charlie called him (meaning "good," compare hyu-skookum-man in the artificial lingua franca invented by the Kootnai Indians), a little blond kid about five years old, the son of their cook; but his mother, a widow, was not willing to give him up; and when, later on, she married again and *was* willing, Nancy said No. Ever since then they had talked at intervals of having Doc Longeway find them a baby; and now, perhaps with some premonition that his own life was not as safe as it had always seemed, Charlie began agitating the subject again. This would be 1916 with Charlie fifty-two.

He wanted a girl, his argument being, "I'm older than you and I'll die first. If we adopt a boy he'll light out across country as soon as he grows up, or go to jail or something; but a girl stays home till she's married, and she'll be company for you."

But Nancy wanted a boy. Nothing happened for months —perhaps a whole year or more—and then, quite suddenly, they adopted a baby only a few weeks old and christened him Jack.

Later, when they first went to California, my mother visited the Russells in Pasadena. By then Jack was three or four years old and stood no nonsense from Charlie—who, of course, spoiled him—but was already sufficiently wise in the ways of the world to hop around very lively when Nancy indicated that was the thing to do. We all of us hopped around very lively when Nancy was pacing the quarterdeck.

That last sentence sounds faintly disparaging. What I meant was that Nancy got action out of everyone around her. Nobody could accuse her of driving Charlie, but without her he would have amounted to very little. He might have become as good an artist, but he would never have got anywhere, certainly never have got as far as New York.

But this is unfair to Charlie. He might have been a better artist without Nancy. All we can be sure of is that if left to himself he would never have competed with commercial artists and his development would have been quite different. Not necessarily better or worse but certainly different.

In this book Nancy is at a disadvantage; she appears as just a foil for Charlie. Actually she was very much a person in her own right. She was not only pretty but had great personal charm; all men fell for her, and most women. It was the masterful, overbearing, bossy women who disliked her.

Nancy had one great defect—her blind worship of the Bitch Goddess *Success*. And by success she didn't mean just money.

All the time I was in Montana the Russells drew a steady income from contracts with either Brown & Bigelow or the Osborne Company, then the two biggest calendar outfits in the world.

These contracts paid two thousand—later four thousand —dollars a year and required Charlie to submit four oil paintings of which the company had the right to reject two. They often did reject one or two and always for the same reason—color. The mountains, or the sky, or the haze, or the distance, had too much purple, or the distance was too delicate and wouldn't reproduce. (Color reproduction was not nearly as good then as it is now.) Did this worry, continuing for years—and it was a very real and serious worry— affect Charlie's use of color?

The paintings themselves did not belong to the calendar company; all they bought was the right to reproduce. They returned the originals and Charlie could and did sell them. Their being used as calendars did not seem to affect the sales. These contracts ran for three years each, and Nancy was always able to renew them.

Charlie And Nancy As Partners

Many successful New York artists envied Charlie the security and peace of mind these contracts gave him.

But the biggest credit mark against Nancy's name is that she had Charlie's models cast in bronze. *He* would have been content with wax and plaster—both impermanent —but she insisted on the expense, the worry, and, for a long time, the disappointment, of casting in bronze. Charlie loved to model but was never satisfied with the castings—he wanted more detail.

Critics do not agree with him. Some of them set his bronze much higher than his paintings.

I roused Nancy's ire by remarking that sculpture in the round should be in repose, not violent action. I had read that somewhere.

Said Charlie, "What the kid wants is a wooden cigar-store Indian with lots of red and green and gold, and eye-balls painted chalk white and the eyes glaring."

Charlie himself was a little inclined that way: most of his plaster figures were polychrome. He did however model Nancy a nymph and a frog and paint it bronze green; and they had, up on the stair landing, a big plaque in low relief, colored the same way, which I prefered to most of the real bronzes.

If left to himself, Charlie was not very practical; he would devote just as much care to things not meant to sell. For instance, he took an old-fashioned boys' book of mine, *Frank on the Prairie,* and extra-illustrated, or rather illu-minated it, with chapter headings and tail pieces in ink and watercolor. Most of the figures are quite small, Indians, trappers, animals, less than half an inch high.

He also made me a full sized water color of Attila the Hun—I had been expatiating on how he kept the white men jumping sideways and on his spectacular death by spontan-eous combustion after a five days' drunk—and another of

Parthian Gotarzes with horn-bow and scale armor. Also a crusader in oil. All are mounted and none of them look like Charlie's other work. Then too—but this is a mere sketch—I have a drunken Nero, complete with olive wreath and a brutal grin. Also—another sketch—a Mandrill monkey with livid blue and vermilion at both ends.

But to get back to Nancy. You could see her effect on Charlie all the time, and not merely in his work. When she made him dress for dance or reception and put on his dark blue double-breasted coat and starched white shirt and black silk sash with spreaders in it to keep it from rolling up in a rope as ordinary sashes do—the sash was wide enough to take the place of a vest—Charlie suddenly became a very distinguished personage. Clothes didn't make him—he always had a fine-looking head and a good figure—but they certainly improved him. And when he was wearing that sash he stood up straight; he didn't, as he expressed it, go around with a hump like a buffalo. Nobody who knew him could imagine Charlie dressing up like that of his own accord, and nobody could have made him except Nancy.

Whether or not her activities interfered with his development as an artist, you can certainly say this much for Nancy—she made Charlie a material success.

When one of the ladies of the family had read the proof this far she objected, "You harp continually on Nancy's success but never mention her devotion to Charlie. She *was* devoted: to her he was *the* perfect man. After his death"—for Nancy was the younger and long outlived him—"she tried to keep herself busy by selling pictures, but it was no good. She could sell only pictures she believed in, and the only pictures she really believed in were Charlie's."

⇜§ 24 §⇝

The Twilight Wolf

Kveld-ulf our Norse ancestors called it, the Twilight Wolf, and their last prophecy ends with the ominous sentence, "When the Wolf comes to Asgard."

Asgard, you know, means God-guard, the place where the Gods are safe. When the Wolf comes to Asgard, the Gods fall and that age, the age of innocence, comes to an end. Gotterdammerung the Germans called it but the Norse called it Ragnarok, the Twilight of the Gods—twilight before the night which will have no end.

1916 was my last summer at Lake McDonald and full of omens—had I had the wit to recognize them—that it *was* the last.

But I was young then and had no philosophy and didn't know an omen when I saw it, not even when it turned on me and glared, green-eyed, in the twilight and popped its jaws.

Instead of saying, "Here, embodied in beast form and quick and agile and more than a little terrifying, is a presentiment of the years which now will run beside me to the end, yea, run away with me," all I said was, "My gosh, it's a wolf!"

A wolf in a cage is not very impressive; a police dog or a mastiff look more dangerous; even a wolf on the prairie, though exciting, does not awe you; but a timber wolf in the timber is quite different. He is where he belongs, you are where you don't, and the stage is set in his favor. With one bound he can disappear in the wings, you can't; all you can do is walk—you'd better not run—and wonder on which side he is following you; being a wolf he certainly will follow.

The trail along the lake ran right in front of Charlie's cabin as straight as the string of a bow. Joining it at both ends and bent like a bow, a second trail curved up over the hill, an old abandoned trail no longer used by anyone but me. Full of supper and energy, it was my habit in the long northern evening to hurry, rejoicing, up over the hill and along the crest and beat twilight back to the lake. An exultant hurry which, though I didn't know it then, was really a sort of hymn to youth and health. A hymn without words, beaten out by my blood and my feet on the trail, my own feet running away with me.

As summer deepened down into autumn and the evenings shortened, I had to go faster and faster, almost run, to get down again to the water before dark. Even after it was pit-black in the timber, there was still a faint glow of light along the lake.

That particular evening I had climbed the hill and gone along the crest to where the trail joined the Oil Road—so called because it once led up to oil fields in Canada—and there, in the road, I walked right up on a wolf, the first time I ever saw one in the timber. In that light he looked almost black. He also looked very big.

I saw him but he didn't see me. He was standing alert, side toward me but with his head turned away, watching the road intently as if expecting something to come up around the bend. The wind was from him to me, my moccasins made no noise and he didn't hear me.

Before I could decide what to do he suddenly turned—without looking back—and trotted quickly down the road and around the bend. As soon as he was out of sight I hurried after him, running on my toes. I was tremendously excited—what they call buck-fever.

The oil road, zig-zagging steeply down the hill, this way, that way, bends every few yards, and when I reached the second bend there he was, still trotting ahead of me and just about to disappear around the third.

As soon as he did I ran after him.

I followed him like that around four bends but at the fifth I pulled up with a jerk—he had stopped and was standing not ten feet ahead, still intent on the road below.

But this time either I made a noise or the wind had changed. He suddenly turned his head and looked back over his shoulder and saw me. He made a startling mask, his prick ears, his laughing jaws, his lolling tongue; in that light, or lack of it—for it was getting darker every minute—his eyes were not yellow as they should be, but as green as glass, and perfectly round and apparently without pupil.

For a long moment we stared at each other, startled; and then, without warning, not even snarling, he suddenly popped his jaws—it made a surprising noise—and turned like a flash and jumped over a big down tree alongside the road, and instantly and utterly vanished. This without any noise whatever except those popping jaws.

He had jumped over that high log as lightly as a deer, just bounced, and the blackness beyond it swallowed him.

Then *I* got worried. I couldn't see him and I couldn't hear a thing. He might be right on the other side of the log, or he might have already made off through the timber. But I had a notion he had not gone far and that though I couldn't see him he could still see me. And that his eyes were still green, and his jaws still laughing.

213

I hated to turn my back on him, but it was the only thing to do.

I went all the way down the road, bend after bend—the deeper down I went the darker it got but I was afraid to hurry—sure all the time that he was trotting silently alongside, and though I knew that wolves do not jump grown people I was not a bit easy. It made my heart bound when at last—through a sudden gap in the feathery black branches —I saw the pale gleam of the lake.

This was the second time that I had seen the water through the branches, and both times it meant safety, as if it said, "This way out of the wood."

That was my only encounter with the wolf; I never saw him again in his beast shape. Not much of an adventure, you will say, but it excited me.

When the wolf came to Charlie it took a different form. Perhaps he had met it before in a wolf's shape—this time it came as a spider.

Again it was evening, though not quite twilight. We were coming in single file through the timber back of the cabin with Nancy as always ahead (like Joseph of Arimathea —"Joseph who algates went tofore") and suddenly, in the shadowy brown silence—I remember distinctly that the light was brown—the woods, the light, the leaves, everything brown—suddenly, in that shadowy peace and silence—we were tired, nobody was talking—the slope as slippery as glass and as steep as a roof, and Charlie's high heels betrayed him. He slipped on the pine needles and wrenched his back badly and got a heavy fall—he went down with a crash of broken twigs. It startled all of us.

Nancy was frightened. She thought nothing of it when she keeled over in a faint, but Charlie was different.

The Twilight Wolf

We got him up, first sitting, then up on his feet, but he was too shaken to walk alone—perhaps he suspected he hadn't slipped, that something else struck him down—and Nancy and I half led him, half supported him the rest of the way to the cabin, the others trailing along behind, exclaiming.

We had supper and though Charlie handled himself very gingerly he seemed to be all right but unnaturally silent, as if listening to himself—listening to the machinery running down?—and we turned in hours earlier than usual. Along in the night, about two o'clock Nancy shook me out of a sound sleep and I heard the most horrible moaning. It filled the whole house.

For a moment I didn't know what it was—a painful, struggling gasp for breath and then a long groan of agony. It made your blood flow back.

I got up, quaking, and in the circle of lamplight saw what there was to see—Charlie lying sideways in bed, twisted up in a knot. He couldn't unbend, he couldn't talk; every breath was an agony. He wouldn't answer questions —just that horrible moaning, which filled the whole room. You imagined it streaming out the window—like a stream of mist—and winding away through the woods;—flowing, waist-high, through the woods, a white river of pain.

We all thought him dying.

Under Nancy's fierce direction I pulled on pants and sweater and moccasins, and went down and slid out the canoe and paddled across the lake—flat, waveless, utterly still—imagining that moaning long after I had stopped hearing it—and landed at the Post Office and pounded on the door—made the whole clearing echo—till Apgar raised a window and threw down the key; and I opened and went in, striking matches, and found the phone and wound it up— you had to wind it like a coffee-grinder—and called Columbia

Falls and the nearest doctor. The nearest doctor, but he was miles away and would have to come by train to Belton, and then by stage to Apgar, and then by boat across the lake.

When at last I got him—I wish I could remember his name—he was very nice about it and promised to catch the earliest train and be at the lake by eight.

There was no more to do. I left the key inside and the door unlocked and went down to the beach.

Paddling over, I had been in too much hurry to notice things, but going back—and afraid to get there, expecting to find Charlie dead—I had time to take in the utter and absolute silence of the whole country, not a breath of air, not a ripple on the lake, not a single stir in the timber.

The only sign of life was when half way over I saw some small creature—a muskrat maybe—swimming straight for the other shore, three miles away.

As I drew near camp I saw first a pale speck—the buffalo skull up on its pole to mark the landing—and then the cabin, or at least its light through the branches; and as soon as I landed and pulled up the canoe and stepped off the noisy pebbles onto the needles, I heard Charlie moaning. A ghastly sound, and now it filled the whole country; it didn't seem to come from the house, it seemed to come out of the woods.

Nancy heard the clatter of the pebbles and came down to meet me with a swinging lantern. I told her about the doctor and we went in.

Charlie was lying there more twisted up than ever. We were quite sure he was dying and we didn't know what to do. At intervals Nancy tried to give him whiskey but he couldn't drink; his jaws were set like lockjaw.

"Rigor mortis!" I thought, and after that I couldn't think anything else—Rigor mortis, Rigor mortis, it was like a tune in time to Charlie's moaning.

The Twilight Wolf

It came morning at last and time for the first stage, and I went over in the rowboat—Nancy wouldn't let me use the canoe—and got the doctor; and the very first thing he did was to take out his needle and give Charlie a shot. Even after all these years I remember the blissful fashion in which the moaning slowed down and died away. You could hear and see him floating off into that heavenly state, release from pain. His bent back straightened a little, his twisted arms and legs relaxed, and he sighed and began to breathe even with ease.

I don't recall what else the doctor did, if anything, and we began talking about it. At first we blamed it on the fall, then somebody remembered that the day before something had bitten Charlie, he supposed a spider. There are plenty of spiders in the pine forests and once in a while you see a monster. But the doctor called it erysipelas and wouldn't commit himself as to what caused it and whether or not it could come from a spider's bite.

He said however that Charlie could travel and would be better off at home, so we broke camp that same day—an exhausting business without Charlie's help—and caught the night train to Great Falls. Although I didn't know it, that was my last sight of Lake McDonald.

Charlie got over the bite—or whatever it was—and told me with an air of profound discovery, "You know, till that night, I never knew what a headache was. I supposed women had them—women have all sorts of things—but when a man complained of headache I thought it was just a sympathy play, that he wanted somebody to cry over him. But that night I found out!"

He had lived more than half a century and never had a headache until then.

⤜§ 25 §⤛

The Big Mural At Helena

Charlie had made colored illustrations for *Indian Why Stories* by the poet Frank Linderman. Frank, somewhat younger than Charlie, a quick, energetic, impatient fellow, had led an active life, steamboating on the Great Lakes in early days, then hunting, trapping and prospecting out west, and, as the country settled up, graduating into politics, literature and insurance. In which last he did so well that he was able to retire at forty-five and build himself a place on Swan Lake. Now, when I knew him, middle-aged, he had become a dapper, alert-looking person in nose-pincher glasses, still quick, still energetic and still impatient. His impatience was not diminished when he ran for election and was defeated by Jeanette Rankin, the first woman in Congress.

He was greatly interested in the Indians and went at his own expense to Washington to try and do something for the landless and starving Crees.

Frank was not the sort of person you could ignore; he had plenty of political connections and stirred up quite a commotion, but, as one of the Senators told him, "Mr. Linderman, these people talk about helping the Indian but they're not going to *do* anything because the Indian has no vote."

And they didn't do anything.

Frank returned, embittered, to Montana and solaced himself by persuading Charlie to go on a flat-boat trip down the Missouri from the Lower Falls to Fort Benton, a part of the river on which there are now no steamers nor any traffic at all. There were four of them, Charlie, Frank, Doc Murgatroyd of Helena, and a fourth person whom I never saw and whose name I do not remember.

They had a small outboard motor which sometimes worked and sometimes didn't—motors were new then and not very dependable—but the main idea was to drift with the current all day and camp ashore at night.

Frank did the organizing and provided the boat but the Doctor supervised the provisions and along with the food he brought plenty of soap. When it came to stowing the cargo they discovered that either it was more bulky than they had figured or the scow was less roomy; and about every third item they handled seemed to be soap.

"I didn't know this was a business trip," said Charlie. "Doc must be starting a laundry."

"Hell!" said Frank at his most impatient, "that's too much soap!" and threw it overboard.

It turned out to be—like Kipling's Just-so Tiger—All-the-Soap-There-Was, and they went the rest of the way without washing.

Then there was Dr. Murgatroyd's pillow. He brought it for his sole use, being a luxury-loving cuss, but in the confusion of embarking somebody ignited it with a cigarette. Instead of blazing up in one bright flame, as you would expect a pillow to do—the living coal sank into it like seed—like spiritual seed into the soul—and it began to burn internally, smoking, smouldering, and stinking; and the four of them proved quite unable to quench it. They sat on it and smothered it and poured cupfulls of water into the burning part and finally dunked the whole thing in the river and then hung it up on twigs in the bow to dry. It never dried enough to use as a pillow, but, like the ever-burning lamp in a magician's tomb, it never went out. Days later they would suddenly notice a thin plume of smoke streaming up from the pillow's heart. Frank, an unbeliever, called it the Burning Heart of Jesus.

Thus with a smoking pillow to guide them—and no soap —they descended the lonely reaches of the Missouri with its winding bed, its undercut mud bluffs—they saw two of them fall—and on the banks no sign of civilization except an occasional deserted shack, the abandoned home of some starved-out dryland farmer. They didn't see any cattle, or even sheep.

"You'd almost think," said Charlie on his return, "that the country is really going back to the Indians. It looks exactly as empty as when I came here a generation ago. Emptier even, because then there weren't any deserted houses."

In other words, what the white man's celebrated energy has done is kill off the Indians, the antelope and the buffalo; slash the forests, gut the mines, break the prairie sod, destroy the grazing (thousands of miles of good grassland destroyed forever) and turn natural pasture land into a dustbowl. Which accomplished, the white man moved on, triumphant, to other things.

Perhaps that's what the dinosaurs did with their world, and you know what happened to them.

A cantankerous Briton who had lived in America must have had us in mind when he wrote:

By the rubbish in our wake
And the noble noise we make,
Oh be sure we're going to do some wondrous things.

Ostensibly he was describing the Banderlog, the Monkey People, but really he meant us—whom else could he mean?

220

"However," said Charlie, who wasn't thinking about the Banderlog, "we saw what I haven't seen for years—dawn over the prairie, and not a house or a factory or a fence in sight. And gorgeous sunsets on the river." That's one advantage of traveling in a scow; you can't help seeing the dawn—it wakes you up.

This trip, less than a week long, had a lasting effect on Charlie's art. All the years since he married he had been living in town, and in a town, no matter how small, you never see the whole circle of the horizon, never get the full splendor of the sky and dawn and sunset—which are horizon matters—you get only the blaze of noon. But now—as if in his youth when he lived on the range, he had not been able to appreciate what he saw, or not able to communicate it— now he began to paint those ruddy glowing sunsets with Indians figures, not white men, which, to me at least with my barbarous taste for color, have more magic in them than all his previous pictures. Especially one where the Medicine Man on horseback, with arms outstretched, Sings the Sun Down. Charlie nowhere tells what song he sang but looking at the picture you can imagine that gutteral chant, repeated over and over until the sun is gone.

Some years earlier (1909) Charlie had been invited to the Coeur d'Alaine country to help round up the last big herd of buffalo on what was then the Flathead Indian Reservation. The Reservation—promised to the Indians and their children for "as long as the sun shines and the grass grows" —was about to be opened to the whites.

Peblo, the half breed who owned the buffalo—eight hundred head—asked Uncle Sam to leave him a strip of range or else buy the herd. The U. S. Government—vividly interested in free land—was not interested in buffalo. The Canadian Government *was* interested, and grabbed them at two hundred and fifty dollars a head. (Afterward the U. S.

set aside a pasture not thirty miles from Peblo's range and began a new herd with *four* buffalo, two of them given by Conrad of Great Falls.) Charlie camped with the Canucks who came to get the herd and was delighted to see wild horses still running loose.

Peblo's riders were all either breeds or full bloods—a wild looking bunch—and with much hard riding they drove three hundred buffalo into a big timber trap; but when they saw they were cornered most of them broke back and got across the river. Said Charlie in a letter to Philip Goodwin, "I wish you could have seen them take the river   they hit the water on a ded run   that river was a tapyoker for them an they left her at the same gate - - -"

The riders went to bed that night with one hundred and twenty in the trap, but they woke up with only one cow: the rest had climbed the cliff and got away. Next day they caught only six, and then the first big autumn snowstorm made them call off the round up till next summer.

In the end, of course, the Canadians got the herd and shipped them up across the Line, where they soon paid for themselves and began paying dividends.

At Coeur d'Alaine—but they pronounce it Coordaleen— there were many French Canuck halfbreeds, the children and grandchildren of the original buffalo runners; and Charlie told one of the oldest that he ought to write his memories. "Oh couldn't do *that!*" said the oldster, "they might hang me, you know."

Lots of good stories must go untold for that reason.

The oldster's son had two daughters, Marie and Isabel, who had been to school. Marie played the piano, Isabel sang. Her father, who, in his Franco-American English always put an H on her name, was very proud of her singing, "*H*isabel, what song you goin' to sung now?"

It made Charlie wish he had a couple of daughters.

One of the riders on this round-up was a full-blood, a big, tall, fine-looking Indian called Almost-a-woman. When they had been camping together a few days, Charlie felt well enough acquainted to ask how he got such an odd name, he being one of the least effeminate looking men around there.

"When I was born," said the buck, "the old women who were helping my mother came out of the lodge and told the tribe that it was a girl baby, and it was two or three days before my manhood came out; so they called me Almost-a-woman."

Charlie came home from this, his last round-up, with a lost feeling that another part of the world he knew had gone over the Line with the herd.

In these, his middle-aged years, Charlie went on an expedition of some kind every autumn after he got back from his summer camp on Lake McDonald. Once he and Emerson Hough went up north, way up the Canadian rivers almost to the Barren Grounds, with a wealthy Englishman. And once, but this was much earlier—either 1905 or 1907—Caspar Whitney, editor of *Outing*, sent him to Mexico to illustrate an article in that magazine, and while there he stayed for several days at the immense Don Liuz Terrazo ranch which was said to be the largest in the Americas, but I have since heard that there are several even larger in Argentina. It was when he stopped at our house in St. Louis on his way home that I first saw, in a water color of a narrow Mexican street, the new word Cafeteria (but Charlie called it Cafet*ereeah*, which is how he had heard it in Mexico). Charlie claimed he learned to talk Mexican. When he went into a restaurant he always ordered, real loud and firm, "Dos wave-os *boilos!*" and they always understood. But he got awfully tired of boiled eggs.

Except illustrations, Charlie painted very few Mexican subjects. He felt he hadn't been there long enough to know the land or the people—and he didn't like to paint what he didn't know.

(I have two—the only Aztec pictures Charlie ever painted. One, unfinished and unsigned, shows Ahuitzotl in sandals, breechclout, green cloak and a gorgeous Quetzal headdress, sitting on the edge of a stone throne—not a very good throne either, he couldn't sit back, there's no room for his feathers—and before him Ixlilton, very proud and villainous, who has just stabbed Chaltzantzin. This picture has never been exhibited, and never will be.

The other—started by me—shows the chiefs meeting before the gate of Tenochtitlan, and I had the city wall drawn right across the paper from edge to edge. "Don't do that!" said Charlie. "Don't divide a picture in layers like a cake. And don't show Aztecs in white nightshirts like Greeks and Romans. An Indian—*any* Indian, even if he was an Emperor or a High Priest—would certainly paint something on his shirt." And he got so interested that he finished it himself. This picture, too, is not for *hoi polloi*. (You know what the Scots say on that subject, "Never show unfinished work to fools and children.")

Speaking of pictures not in his usual line, while I was in Great Falls, Charlie painted Brother Van (Van Orsdel, the Methodist missionary) in long coat and big hat, on horseback, shooting buffalo. It's not a large picture but Charlie worked harder on it than most, trying to make it look as Brother Van must have looked when he was young. Brother Van was delighted but Charlie was not. "It's off my range," said he, "I'm no portrait painter."

Of course, it was not a portrait; and Charlie had painted many Indian heads—including Chief Medicine Whip of *Counting Coup*—but he seldom painted white men. His pen sketches of himself rolling a cigarette are excellent and so is his oil of the night-wrangler in a slicker (himself) coming back to camp for coffee in *When Laugh Cures Lonesome*. The Adams-Britzman biography says that Charlie painted portraits of Jim Bridger, Will Rogers, and Douglas Fairbanks (as d'Artigan) but I have never seen them.

Another thing out of his usual line was to paint a whole set of lunch plates for Nancy, on each a girl in costume—Indian, Mex, Chinese, Italian, etc. It was the fashion right then for women to paint china, so Josephine Trigg "pounced" a background in shell-blue and put a gilt edge on the plates and had them fired. I also painted a plate for my Aunt Sue with an Egyptian scarab—but in Missouri they call it a tumble-bug. You see them in the dust of the country roads tumbling over a neat little ball of dung which contains their eggs. A nice subject, but some people don't like bugs on plates. If Charlie's set has survived the smash and breakage of half a century they must have gone to Josephine on Nancy's death. I don't think Charlie signed them.

All this amused Charlie—and wasted his time, and paid no bills—but now, suddenly, like smoke on the horizon—signal smoke, at first a few puffs, then a tall column, an exclamation mark!—here came the chance to paint a really big picture, the biggest picture of his life. To wit, a proposed mural, a wall-painting, for the State Capitol at Helena, Montana.

As the wind blew the exclamation became a question mark. It was to be competitive, artists from all over would be eligible, especially those who had already painted murals—could Charlie get it?

Nancy thought so but Charlie had his doubts, though the subject was right up his alley—Lewis and Clark meeting the Blackfoot Indians. The first historic event—white man's history—in Montana.

Charlie had read the famous Journals and knew where they had met—"Ross' Hole up in the Bitter Root Valley."

Charlie knew the country but it wasn't enough; he and Nancy went there.

It was fall of the year. It rained and misted while they were there, and that's how Charlie decided to paint it with the rain clearing. He made sketches of the country and of the mountains which form the natural background.

"What does mural mean anyhow?" asked Charlie.

But I knew all the answers, "A mural painting, you know, like a—like a—like a mural crown!"

Well, what else *is* mural?

"Now that helps a lot," said Charlie. "It makes everything just as clear as mud."

He was worried. He had never painted any murals and this would be twenty-six feet long by twelve high—many times bigger than anything he had ever attempted, and the foreground figures—the Indians on horseback—would be almost lifesize. But Nancy was sure he could do it.

I put in my two bit's worth by informing them that he would have to paint it right on the plaster; that the plaster had to be fresh and just enough of it spread for what he could cover in one day; then if at evening any plaster was left unpainted it would have to be chipped off the wall and a new coat put on next morning; and, finally, that instead of oil he would have to mix his paints with egg.

I had gone down to the Library and read how they used to do it.

"Egg!" said Charlie. "Squeeze it out of the hen, I suppose, instead of out of a tube. Well, you can come along and hold the hen. When I holler, 'Egg!' you squeeze her."

It looked for a while as if he might not get the contract. Some Montana senators wanted to import a New York artist. John Alexander is the only name I remember: he specialized in murals and had a number already in different cities. Much as he disliked it, Charlie had to go to Helena and appear in person before the Senate and fight to get the contract. His argument ran, "If you want cupids and angels and Greek goddesses, give this New Yorker the job. If you want a western picture, give it to me."

This was a real ordeal for Charlie, who hated to brag about his work or disparage another painter.

In the end he got the contract—ten thousand dollars. (Years later Ed Doheney, the oil millionaire of the Teapot Dome scandal, paid him forty thousand for a mural, a frieze around the walls of his breakfast room.)

After all the State Capitol mural was not painted directly on the plaster but on a specially made canvas so large that the roof of the log cabin studio had to be raised, and Charlie worked on the upper half of the picture from movable steps with a railed platform five feet square at the top. He had to use special colors and a brush as big as a house painter's. An expert came from Chicago to stretch the canvas, and, when it was finished, take it down and roll it and hang it in the Capitol building. An anxious business for everybody.

Montana was proud of the mural; other states were envious but praised it, and it wasn't until years later—long after Charlie's death—that anyone disparaged it in my presence.

Then a New York woman, interested in modern art and acquainted with Charlie's work, asked in what style it was painted.

I described it from memory: in the foreground the Indians pulling up their horses; in the middle distance the two exporers and their men and Sacajaweeah, the Sho-sho-nee girl who acted as guide and interpreter, and York, the first Negro the plains Indians had ever seen or heard of— he attracted much more attention than the two leaders.

("Ho-ho-hay-eeee! Hy-u skookum man—*black!*" They rubbed him and looked at their thumbs to see if the black would come off. Several tribes offered him women. Naturally York refused. Then again, maybe he didn't. The two leaders got very jealous—York was collecting all the sample fornication.) I told all this, omitting the sample part, and as far as I could remember, I described the background.

"But the style?" the New York woman insisted.

I answered as best I could: no, it was not painted flat; no, it wasn't just a frieze; no, it was not symbolical—no allegorical goddesses of liberty and progress, no westward stars of empire, no balances and scales of justice, no cornucopias and horns of plenty: no crowded jumble in the one picture of Indians, explorers, missionaries, cowboys, miners, wagon-trains, railroads, automobiles and thrashing machines; no allegory of any kind, no symbolism; just a plain picture, as real as Charlie could make it, of the Blackfoot Indians getting their first look at Lewis and Clark.

"In other words," said the New Yorker, summing up, "it was just a regular Russell canvas writ large."

"What's wrong with that?" I asked.

Apparently everything was wrong with it: it was just everything a mural shouldn't be.

"But," I pointed out, "it's what the Montana people wanted. They would neither have liked nor understood anything symbolic, and had he painted it flat they would have thought they were cheated."

In my ignorance I supposed she objected to Charlie and would have preferred some other painter.

"Oh it isn't *that!*" she explained. "Any other American would have been just as hopeless—look at the public building atrocities the New Deal produced and called them murals! And as for Alexander—!"

The Big Mural At Helena

I didn't get it and I don't yet, but I was shaken.

And now we come to the crux of the matter, the question which plagues all western painters—indeed all American painters—was Charlie a real artist or just a story-teller?

What makes Americans always doubt their own artists? Whence this queer modesty? Why do we let the Europeans lay down the law in Art?

Is there one definite test to which you can put the artist?

⋖§ 26 §⋗

Injun-Jo Galoopie

"Korzouf, they said, had neither father nor mother: he was born of the desert and to the desert he would return. He with El the son of O and Chang the Wilful came on shaggy northern camels out of the waste and rode across the grasslands. Eight days they rode and on the ninth they came in the afternoon to that crest called Seeing, and went thereon and saw the golden city and the golden river under the golden sky. But they did not see Alodai in the reeds."

Alodai was the Lewdworm.

If you read further in the epic fragment you learn that Chang had been there before and knew the city was built of mud, and, like the river and the sky, looked golden only because the sun was shining.

The artist should be like Korzouf, without father or mother, and well aware that in the end he will return to the desert from which he came, but none the less crossing the grasslands with a high heart and seeing—which is to say creating—the golden city. For you must see before you can create; the Kosmocrators saw before they built. And the true Artist is a Kosmocrator.

But he must not only see; he must also select. Blake, for instance, who saw but would not, or could not, select, created not a Kosmos but a Chaos.

In the unfinished epos of the Grail, Messire Gawain, Arthur's best nephew, came to the Grail Castle and sat at the ritual feast and saw the procession of the weeping women but did not see the Cup. Why? Wearied with this world's work he fell asleep; and so, when he woke, was unable to ask the healing—and revealing—question. How could he ask of what he had not seen?

The true artist must not be too busy with this world's work, he must keep awake to the Cup, he must solder the Broken Sword, he must see the City.

Was Charlie Russell a true artist, had he seen the Golden City? Did he ask the healing question?

To which the ancient critics, as old as Egypt, the Accusers of the Dead, to whom every man must show his work at last, answer with a laugh.

If *they* condemn him, then let us arise and slay Charlie Russell, the false artist; dismember him as he deserves. And having slain him on the altar of his own incompetence, burn him to ashes. And from the ashes do as the alchemists did —or tried to do—and, as sundry Eastern artists have actually done—the enduring Sons of Han, the People of Yamoto— extract Essence.

But was there any real essence to Charlie's art? Here the Accusers laugh twice.

But—to leave the Assesors in the Court of Osiris—the real proof of the painter is what effect his painting has upon the Artist Everyman.

If Everyman looks at the picture and praises it and passes on and nothing happens, it may be a good picture or it may not; it isn't magic. But if whole months or years or decades later the memory of that picture unites with something else which Everyman has seen or felt or heard, and comes forth in a new form—not just that picture, not just the something else, but both combined—which is to say if the sleeping artist in Everyman awakes, why then the

231

painter has not painted in vain. What comes in a new shape could not have come in just that shape had he not sowed the seed.

Charlie, the most unmystical of men, at least in all outward seeming (but how do I know what that stern mask concealed, for Charlie's face in repose was both stern and grim), Charlie who never indulged in high-flown talk and who had, I think, no sense of the supernatural—which seems odd in an artist—would read this over and grunt, and read it again and say, "But what does this stuff mean—does it mean anything?"

Not long ago I showed some Russell reproductions to a modern girl, a New Yorker born and bred, who has never been as far west as Niagara Falls.

She leafed through them with rapidly waning interest and floored me flat by announcing, "But they have no social implications."

A criticism that had never occurred to me.

"And was he a woman hater? Not one picture has a woman in it!"

"They're historically important," I protested. "Charlie painted what he had seen and taken part in. And they're authentic—the dress, the horse-furniture, the look of the country before the nesters came—every detail is right."

"Oh, I suppose it's real Americana," she conceded. "And he doesn't seem to romanticize the Indians—they look savage and brutal enough. And a lot of the white men look dirty!"

"They were not a tidy bunch. They hadn't heard about B.O. and that a gentleman changes his linen every day. They started the round-up with the clothes they had on and a slicker and a couple of blankets, and came back, months later, in the same shirt. When they struck a river they took a bath—if it happened to be hot weather."

"I suppose you could call it John Ree," said the girl.

"Who?" Evidently John was some painter I hadn't heard about.

But she had already gone back to her social implications.

"How can an artist claim any real significance, any lasting importance, unless his art contains some criticism, overt or implied, of the world he lives in?"

"But Charlie was not a critical sort of person. He took things as they came and painted them that way."

"Photographic!" said the girl, and shut me up like a book. "A camera doesn't criticize either—it just records."

I repeated this conversation to a mutual acquaintance.

"Oh *her!*" he said, "that social implication stuff dates her just as much as Charlie Russell's pictures date him. And now that the Republicans are in, she and her kind are as out of date as Charlie. Moreover get this—the front-rank artists, Homer, Shakespeare and so forth, have always recorded, not criticized. It's only the second-raters, like Dickens, who set up as reformers and preach crusades. Christ—and St. Paul—started a new religion; Peter founded the Church: would you lower them to a level with the men, centuries later, who preached the first crusade? Of course, the real artist prepares the way for the second- and third-rank people by boiling down what he records. His final product—though he may not intend it—deals not with individuals but with types: the gist of the matter."

"You mean he Extracts Essence?"

"Exactly, though I wouldn't put it that way."

"But that's just what I was afraid Charlie didn't do!"

"You're not an artist and so not qualified to judge. Wait till a full generation has passed and then let the current artists decide about Charlie. You'll find he ranks up with the best."

He smoked for a minute and then left off defending Charlie to attack me, "Did you ever hear Charlie Russell use that catchword about extracting essence?"

"No, I doubt if he'd ever heard it."

"You'd be a better judge if you'd never heard it. Come to my place tomorrow and I'll give you proof that Charlie Russell was not only an artist but a catalyst. A catalyst, you know," he added improvingly—I suppose I looked kind of blank, "is an agent which without being changed itself precipitates changes in others; it clarifies the saturated solution, precipitates it in crystals—crystal clear. Charlie, or one of Charlie's pictures, did just that for a man who was not an artist. What resulted was a very queer crystal indeed."

I didn't know what he meant so we met as arranged and he showed me the following fragment, explaining, "The man who wrote this—not a professional writer—had seen, and entirely forgotten, Charlie's picture *Big Sickness;* he had also read, and forgotten, Mark Twain's account of the halfbreed Injun Joe. Now, years later, the two suddenly combined and produced a third figure, a piece of private mythology, which, whatever it meant to the writer, would certainly have surprised both Mark Twain and Charlie Russell."

He wouldn't say who the writer was, so I was at liberty to draw my own conclusions.

"If this is meant for Missouri dialect," I objected, "I don't think much of it."

"Neither does the writer, but that's the way it came."

"Came?"

"Yes, it just came to him like an inspiration. Now here's the queer part: the writer isn't interested in Daniel Boone and hadn't thought about Mark Twain or Charlie Russell for months, but one night, apropos of nothing—he was worrying about something else—this occurred to him and so impressed him that he wrote it down. It came piecemeal, a part at a time, and took three days. Read it and see what you think."

It was headed *Injun-Jo Galoopie.*

When Dan'l Boone came here from Kaintuk he was goin' thru woods in the swamp-east part of the State, an' he heard a noise, way off, first like fightin' an' then like complainin'; so he went that a-way, cautious-like an' saw a big tall feller in buckskin, leanin' up against a tree, ankle-deep in the swamp. An' he was busy as a bear at a ant-heap pullin' injun arrers out of himself, an' complainin' all the time, "Misery! Misery!"

Dan'l asked who he was an' what he called this part of the country but Jo jus' kept sayin' "Misery! Misery!"

That's how Missouri got its name. An' it's been a good place to come from but a miserable place to live in ever since.

Well, Dan'l pulled a couple more arrers out of him an' took him back to camp an' give him his first drink of likker.

It put Jo out like a light. He took one big drink an' fell over back'ards, an' tho they poured water on him an' dragged him around they couldn't bring him to. They thought he was a croppy, so they drug him out on the dump. The buzzards weren't havin' any, an' the first bird to take a pick at him was a red-headed woodpecker, who must a been pretty desperate.

But he was a wise little peckerwood. One bite was enough. As soon as he could fly again he flew up on a tree an' shook the fleas off an' said:

> "Oh Oh tastes like crow,
>   smells like skunk—
>   it's Injun-jo."

An' he was the first Missourian.

Them days the Injuns lived here in Missouri, an' havin' no wife to cook for him Jo took up with one of their gals what the missionaries had christened Anna. She come from down south, an' after Jo disappeared, so sudden an' tragic-like, she an' her folks went flatboat down river to New Orleens, an' that's how Lousyanna got its name.

Jo, like I tell you, was a squaw-man, an' he an' Lousy-Ann had a bunch of no-good kids. They wouldn't work. They wouldn't do nothin' 'cept eat an' sleep an' fight an' gamble an' go huntin' an' drink corn likker.

Jo used to lick 'em a lot 'cept when they ganged up an' licked him. They'd tree the old man like a possum an' then shy rocks at him. That's how he got so good at dodgin'.

But they'd nick him, sooner or later, an' make him holler, an' his wife would come, a-cussin', an' tear into 'em with a wash-pole an' there wouldn't be ary hog-waller in the hull county without one of Jo's kids in it.

That's how all Missouri people got to takin' a bath every Satady night, 'cept, of course, in fly-time an' durin' the winter. In winter it's too cold, an fly-specks show up worse on you when you're clean than when you ain't.

Speakin' of specks, Jo was a gamblin' man whenever he had any money. Them days dice was marked any old way, but Jo had his private set fixed so that the top an' bottom numbers always come out seven. That's the ony way he'd bet—top an' bottom she adds up seven.

Dan'l Boone had a balky mare an' one day when he was feelin' mean an' she was actin' cusseder than ever, he got mad an' bred her to a dunkey. When the colt came it was all ears an' feet an' Dan'l didn't like the looks of it. He says, "It ain't no horse, an' it ain't no dunkey, an' it ain't no good—give it to Injun-jo."

Jo says thank you kindly, an' called the critter Jack, an' he was the first Missouri mule.

Soon as he could shamble—an' that was right off—Jo tried to ride him. He thought it would save a lot of foot-wear but Jack thought different.

They had quite a argument about it, an' after Jo had been bit all over—an' kicked in between the bites—so that you couldn't tell whether he looked more like a stompin'-lot or fresh chopped hawg-meat, he concluded walkin' was cheaper anyhow—an' a heap healthier—so he give Jack to Lousyanna.

When Jo had been flooded out a dozen times, he 'clared that hereafter he was goin' to live on a hill. But they ain't no hills in the bottomlands, so he planted seed-gravel an' cut sprouts careful with a hoe an' grew him a mound. Then he built him a house with a high-pitched roof to shed the rain, an' he says to the river, "Come on, Swirly, les see what you can do."

Well, high water come an' everybody got drowned out 'cept Jo. He set up on his mound, takin' life easy, an' pretty soon water she crep' up thru the gravel an' washed his house away. Jo straddled up on top with his squaw-lady an' the kids in between.

"Hell!" says Jo, sailin' thru the woods, duckin' branches an' harvestin' up the neighbors' chickens an' houn-dogs, "this here's the sharpest ridgepole I ever rode an' she rides the roughest. Nex' time I'm goin' to build me a house with a nice dry root-cellar up on top to sleep in."

Injun-jo's woman, Lousy-ann, was kind of a ontidy housekeeper, an' one day out in the dog-run she was makin' lye-hominey an' boilin soap, an' between fightin' flys an' quietin' the kids an' drivin' off the wildcats that et the kids, she somehow got the mess mixed up with the mash.

Jo was feelin' mean that mornin' an' jus' for cussedness he spat a jawful of chawin' juice into it to give it a bead; an' that was the first corn likker.

Jo took one drink an' went out, barehanded, an' licked a hull fambly of wildcats what had been eatin' his kids.

After that Jo came back an' took another snort to quiet his nerves—which was standin' up endways all over him like quills on a porky—an' it laid him out so cold that he didn't wake up till civil war days.

Jo looked awful when he woke up, an' he felt worse, an' he couldn't find his fambly, an' the house was jes' a heap of logs with the chimley tumbled down an' the roof caved in; so not havin' nothin' to eat he joined up with Quantrell's gorillas. They was the first gangsters.

The goin' with them was too ruff, even for Jo, so one day when they was squanderin' off thru the woods with Yanks shootin' at 'em from up on the hill an gunboats bangin' an' bombin' away from the river, Jo decided that here was a good chance to sort of un-volunteer himself an' make his get-away.

But he was a big feller an' easy to see—stood seven foot high with his toes out—an' Quantrell caught him sneakin' off thru the woods an' he says, "Look here, Lousy, you joined up an' you can't quit us like that."

"Can't I?" says Jo, innocent-like, "well, then I'll quit you like this!" an' he jumpt in the river. That's how the Mississippi got so yeller—like coffee with milk in it 'stead of cream.

Well, Jo went down river with his nostrils out, like a 'gator down south, an' that's how that point there got its name, Snout-out.

Quantrell an' his gorillas kep' shooting at it, first up one hole, then the other, but the bullets jes' went into Jo's brain an' didn't do no hurt 'cept to make him top-heavy,

like he's been ever since. Pretty soon his big toes was stickin'
up higher than his snout. The gorillas shot holes in 'em, an'
that's what makes him easy to track, an' that's how he got
his other name—Ring-toe Jo.

Here, as suddenly as it began, the "inspiration" ended.
Having emitted this much—entirely unrelated to anything
in which the writer was interested—that door closed. And,
as far as I know, never opened again.

Months later the writer chanced on a magazine article
about Mark Twain and in it a casual reference to Injun Jo.
Until then he had supposed that he—or his subconscious—
invented the name.

"But Charlie has nothing to do with this," I said. "I
don't see why you should blame it on him."

"Well, it was his painting started it."

In other words, he had waked the Artist Everyman.
Everyman, you know, is not a great artist; mostly he just
carves qrotesques at the temple door and never gets inside.

27

The Last Christmas Card And The
Other Rider

Charlie's end was tragic, not because he died—all men must die—but because he died whole years ahead of time and just as he was approaching the peak of his powers.

He killed himself. Not that he committed suicide; he had no inclination that way. He had not tired of life. He was not a modern and had no itch to be out of it all. He had never felt like my Aunt Mildred when she wrote her sister, "I don't think I want to die but it would be nice to be safely dead." Charlie had never felt that way. He loved life; he wanted to go on living.

Nonetheless he killed himself. As in all real tragedy a weakness in his own character destroyed him. Like most very healthy people he feared pain and when they told him, years before the end, that he ought to have an operation, he put it off. Put it off and put it off until it was too late. Thousands of people must do that every year, and always live to regret it. The pity was in Charlie's case that it was quite a simple operation, and, taken in time, not dangerous. Had he taken it he might easily have lived another twenty years. He might be alive today.

And again—as in all real tragedy—the setting, the environment, helped destroy him. His home, his own country which he loved, Montana, so high and so far inland, so far from the life-giving sea, betrayed him. The life-giving, seaweed-growing, iodine-oozing sea. The high prairie and the even higher Rockies did to Charlie what the Tibetan plateau does to the Tibetans and what the Alps and the Andes do to their people—gave him goiter.

When he began to have trouble with his breathing and his heart, the doctors told him what was wrong and what he ought to do, and to do it right away. Charlie refused. Nancy, who ruled him in almost everything, could not rule him in this. Charlie said No.

Perhaps he had already begun to feel the pressure when I left Montana. He had developed what he called a dewlap —such as cattle have, you know—but many people have that and it never occurred to me that it was goiter. All I noticed was that his face had begun to get grim and that he did not seem happy. He was still as amusing as ever and as good a story teller, but he had spells when he didn't want to talk. And once in a while there began to creep into his words a new hardness, almost bitterness, and a new note of cynicism—not about people but about the world. I thought he was just getting older. It never occurred to me that he was sick.

After I left Montana I never saw Charlie again. He wrote only to send Christmas cards, and Nancy wrote only when she wanted me to do something about Charlie's stock in the Parker-Russell M. & M. Co.

She seldom answered questions, and her letters, few and far between, gave such fragmentary information that we in St. Louis knew only that Charlie's reputation was growing steadily and that his pictures sold better and better. For instance, the mural he painted for Edward Doheny, the Teapot Dome oil millionaire, for which, according to rumor, Charlie got forty thousand dollars.

By then my sister was living in New York, and she saw Charlie twice. On their last trip east he and Nancy visited her at Ossining, and she was startled to see him so old

241

and frail and unhappy. This was after a bad attack caused by his heart condition.

In her letters to us in St. Louis, Nancy seldom mentioned Charlie's health, was always optimistic about his recovery; and it was a profound shock to us when we heard that he had been to Rochester to be operated on by the Mayos.

The operation relieved him right away, and Charlie told his stepmother, Mrs. C. S. Russell, "If I had known how easy it was I would have had it years ago."

If only he had known. And if only he had acted in time.

He didn't know—at least I hope he didn't—that though the operation was a success it came too late; that his heart had been under too long a strain; that the doctors gave him only six months to live. They told this to Nancy; they didn't tell Charlie.

Except for goiter there was nothing wrong with him. Had he let them operate just a few years sooner he might be alive today. He didn't and now it was too late.

He went home to Montana to die.

His last Christmas card, which Nancy sent us after his death, is unfinished. It shows Charlie on horseback in the snow, shaking hands with another rider, and the rhyme that accompanies it deals with health and his wish to live. His hope that the worst part of the road was past.

We knew by then who that other rider was.

On Sunday October 24, 1926, Charlie felt well enough to go on quite a long ride. Perhaps it overtired him; perhaps he had just come to the end of the trail. At eleven-forty that evening he had a heart attack and died just before midnight. Nancy and the doctor were with him. He was sixty-four years old.

His father and his brother lived to eighty-four and eighty-six.

The Last Christmas Card And The Other Rider

The funeral was held the following Wednesday at the Episcopal Church of the Incarnation. Young Boy, the Cree Indian whom Charlie had known so long, came from the Reservation. The Elks, the only fraternal order to which Charlie belonged, acted as pall-bearers, and, as he had wished, his body was drawn by horses to Highland Cemetary.

Horace Brewster, the round-up foreman who had been Charlie's boss in the Judith Basin, and Charles Biel, an artist of a new generation, rode behind the hearse and led a riderless horse with Charlie's saddle and spurs.

The city park at Black Eagle Falls was renamed in his honor. His home at 1219 Fourth Avenue North and the four city lots deeded by Nancy now house a small ($75,000) museum.

Nancy moved to Pasadena and built the house Trail's End which she had planned while Charlie was still alive. She died there—May 1940—of heart trouble.

After Charlie's death his pictures began to turn up in all sorts of places. (Also all sorts of forgeries, some of them very crude, turned up. A recent copy of the Montana Historical Society's magazine gives a number of examples.) An "Antelope Hunt" was found painted on the vault doors of a long closed bank in Lewistown, and another, dated 1892, on a safe in a garage which, when Charlie painted it, was a stable.

Charlie's short stories are now beginning to appear in anthologies; the book of his illustrated letters, has been selling ever since he died; reproductions of his work run into hundreds of thousands.

Charlie Russell made his mark, and now there is no one to take his place.

And he was just beginning—"The life so short: the craft so long to learn."

28

Postscript

This book should be called *What I Remember of Charlie Russell* but that would be a clumsy title.

When I began to write it I thought I did not have enough material to make a book, that I would have to pad it, and I intended to tell more about Charlie's home, and, especially, quote his rhymes. Particularly I would include a comic—and highly objectionable—poem about Friar Tuck to accompany a little figure of a monk he made for Mr. Trigg. But the more I wrote the more I remembered, items came in from outside sources, and in the end, instead of padding, I had to cut.

Here are four stanzas, the first two and the last two, of a poem he sent his friend Bob Vaughan.

> Here's to all old timers, Bob,
> They weren't all square it's true,
> Some cashed in with their boots on—
> Good old friends I knew.
>
> Here's to the first ones here, Bob,
> Men who broke the trail
> For the tenderfoot and booster
> Who come to the country by rail.
>
> So here's to my old-time friends, Bob,
> I drink to them one and all,
> I've known the roughest of them, Bob,
> But none that I knew were small.

Postcript

Here's to hell with the booster,
The land is no longer free,
The worst old timer I ever knew
Looks dam good to me.

Also here is a card he sent W. M. Armstrong:

Here's hoping health's the hoss under you
Ahead a long easy ride
Good water and grass
To the top of the pass
Where the trails cross
    The Big Divide

                To you and yours
                From me and mine

                Your Friend,

                    C. M. Russell.

Sources

CHAPTER II

The Bent Family. Allen H. Bent.
Family papers of the Russell, Bent, Parker, Eliot, Kerr, Carr, and Clendenin families.

CHAPTER III

New Mexico Historical Review. Vol. 8, article by Paul A. F. Walters.
The Colorado Magazine. Vol. 12, article by H. L. Lubers.
Harper's Magazine. 1869. (quoted in *Bent's Fort.*)
St. Louis Globe Democrat. May 6, 1838. (Texas attempt to rob Moses Austin's grave.)
Bent's Fort. David Lavender. (This supplied many dates and most details in chapter re the Bents.)
Genealogy of John Eliot descendants. Re C. M. R.'s sister-in-law.)

CHAPTER IV

The Old Gravois Coal Diggins. Mary Joan Boyer.

CHAPTER IX AND CHAPTER XI

Good Medicine. Garden City Pub. Co. (C. M. R. illustrated letters.) Nancy's introduction is quoted re her meeting with C. M. R., his first sight of Helena, and his cooking, "Who is Kid Russell?" etc.
Trails Ploughed Under. Pen & Ink. Doubleday, Page & Co. 1927.

CHAPTER XIX

Riding the High Country. 1933. Pat T. Tucker, Caxton Printers, Caldwell, Idaho.

Piano Jim and the Impotent Vine. By Irvin Cobb. Postscript by Will Rogers, a letter from Mrs. Russell, and a preface by John W. Townsend, Bluegrass Bookshop, Lexington, Ky., 1950.

CHAPTER XXI

The Wilderness Hunter. Theodore Roosevelt. Charlie's version of ghost-bear story.

Pen Sketches or *Western Studies.* No date, very early. Wm. T. Ridgley Co., Falls, Mont.

Studies of Western Life by C. M. R. Copyright, 1890, by Ben Roberts, Cascade, Mont.

CHAPTER XXV

Charles M. Russell, the Cowboy Artist, a biography by Ramon F. Adams and Homer E. Britzman. 1948. Trail's End Press, Pasadena, Calif.